T0317146

THE VERY GOOD MARKETING GUIDE

THE VERY GOOD MARKETING GUIDE

How to Grow Your Business on a Budget

AMY MIOCEVICH

WILEY

First published in 2023 by John Wiley & Sons Australia, Ltd
Level 4, 600 Bourke St, Melbourne Victoria 3000, Australia

Typeset in Tzimmes Medium 10/15pt

© John Wiley & Sons Australia, Ltd 2023

The moral rights of the author have been asserted

ISBN: 978-1-394-18455-2

A catalogue record for this book is available from the National Library of Australia

Cover design by Wiley

Disclaimer
The material in this publication is of the nature of general comment only, and does not represent professional advice. It is not intended to provide specific guidance for particular circumstances and it should not be relied on as the basis for any decision to take action or not take action on any matter which it covers. Readers should obtain professional advice where appropriate, before making any such decision. To the maximum extent permitted by law, the author and publisher disclaim all responsibility and liability to any person, arising directly or indirectly from any person taking or not taking action based on the information in this publication.

Thanks to my family and support network, I was able to bring this book to life whilst also growing my agency and raising a toddler. I thought it couldn't be done, but they proved me wrong. A great deal of love also to my husband: my biggest fan and the world's kindest soul.

TABLE OF CONTENTS

ABOUT THE AUTHOR

Amy Miocevich is the founder of Lumos Marketing, a marketing agency that works exclusively with small businesses.

Over the past decade she's worked with hundreds of Australian SMEs in a consulting and advisory capacity, supporting them to simplify and supercharge their marketing to great success.

The framework developed by Lumos Marketing and documented in this book has helped businesses across Australia to reach their goals and tackle marketing with confidence. It is the only framework in the world that you can turn into a caterpillar by drawing a smiley face in one of the circles.

Amy is surrounded by a network of passionate individuals, both inside her Lumos Marketing team and amongst the clients, professionals and friends she has been fortunate enough to work with over the last decade.

WHY I WROTE THIS BOOK

I've read my fair share of business books: marketing, leadership, culture, strategy and finance books. I am fortunate to have been influenced by the greatest business minds of my time. But when I was growing my own business as a sole trader, I felt like there was a huge void between these amazing stories and theories, and the actions I needed to take for my business, especially when the case studies referenced in my favourite books were about Apple, Google and IBM. I felt so distant from their references of leadership teams, big meetings and high-level strategy plans when it was just me and my laptop and my dining room table.

Australia's small-business economy is growing rapidly, and I truly believe there aren't enough resources out there that help shape small business or give them the practical and simple tools they deserve to make running a business just that little bit easier.

There will always be a place for marketing theory, but unless we create more learning opportunities that bridge theory with action, we will keep seeing the same failure rates in small business that have plagued the industry for the last decade.

I wrote this book to bridge that gap and support business owners on their journey to their dream business and use the best marketing theories in a simple and effective way. It is my hope that this book will make marketing a little bit easier for Australia's biggest dreamers and future world-changers.

INTRODUCTION

Coffee crunch

Shane is a software engineer with a firm in Perth. He's 38, married, has two kids, likes his job, but what he really loves is coffee. He loves playing around with different beans, trying new flavours, blending profiles and learning how it all works. He started off roasting his own beans for his morning hit, but his friends loved his coffee so much, they asked him to sell them some coffee beans.

So he did.

His coffee became so popular, his local café asked him to supply them with some beans. So he did. That got so successful, he thought, 'Why don't I make a go of this and build a coffee roasting business?' Everyone wants coffee, right?

So, he quit his job, bought a premium coffee roasting machine with $40 000 from his mortgage, invested $10 000 on packaging design and branding, and paid $7000 to a website developer to build him an e-commerce website.

It started well, but after five months, a new, much larger coffee roaster negotiated deals with his coffee shops. Deals too good for them to refuse.

To make matters worse, the supply contracts he had negotiated with a major hospitality group were cancelled when the company was bought out by a multinational.

And his new website? He was getting some hits and a few 250 g bag purchases, but not nearly enough to cover his costs.

Now Shane's in deep. He's got a warehouse, stock, overheads to pay and no customers. He's bleeding cash, losing sleep at night, and wondering what he did wrong.

Shane did a lot of things right.

He had a passion for his product. Tick.

He found some early customers. Great.

He invested in some marketing assets and advertising. Awesome.

But he failed to do the thing that would secure a steady supply of new customers.

He failed to do the thing that would guarantee growth and protect his business from competitive threats.

He failed to do the thing that would create a recurring, regular source of income.

Going viral

David is a retired mechanic who loves tinkering with machinery in his backyard warehouse. Over the last ten years, he developed and produced a winch that helps extract trucks and cars when they get stuck in the sand or mud.

It's not your everyday winch. This one hooks onto the wheel instead of the chassis and has 75 per cent more grunt than the others.

Looking to supercharge his growth, David decided to spend $4000 creating a promotional video for the winch. He then uploaded the video to YouTube, spent $5000 on a Google pay-per-click (PPC) campaign to drive traffic to the video and waited with bated breath to see what would happen.

Day one, it racked up 100 views. Day two, 500 views. Day three, 10 000 views. Day four, 70 000 views. By day ten, the video had over two million views. In other words, it went viral.

David was beside himself with joy. This was the beginning of his legacy! This was the start of his new life. The mansion by the sea, the Lamborghini, the first-class travel, the designer suits.

The only trouble was, he didn't sell any winches.

Yes, the views of the video were off the charts, but those views did not translate into sales.

Like Shane, David got a lot right too.

He knew what the customer needed.

He created a unique solution.

He launched a great campaign that went viral.

But he failed to do the thing that would secure a steady supply of new customers.

He failed to do the thing that would guarantee growth and protect his business from competitive threats.

He failed to do the thing that would create a recurring, regular source of income.

Out of office

Helen owns a property management company. She has a small team of property managers and has spent the last decade dedicated to growing her business.

She got to the office by 7 am every weekday and regularly worked late to support her customers.

But as the business grew, Helen began to step out of the day-to-day work of property management (that's what owners did, right?), and started spending her time on things she was really passionate about. She started taking lunch breaks again, going to property seminars, networking with people in the property industry and taking holidays.

And the business was still thriving.

Until it wasn't.

Suddenly, Helen was being notified of contracts being cancelled multiple times a week. Ones from the clients she had been working with for years. The website she had paid $10 000 for wasn't getting her any new customers either. And there were new competitors in her space that had better offerings at a cheaper price.

What was going on?

Like many business owners, Helen was dedicated to her customers.

She had built a name for herself in the industry.

Her business was growing.

And she was ready to start stepping away from the day to day.

But she failed to recognise one important thing.

The thing that would ensure her legacy could exist within her business without her day-to-day involvement.

The thing that would keep her business growing and her customers happy without her presence.

What do Shane, David and Helen all have in common?

None of their marketing is working.

They've got some pieces of the marketing puzzle — they have demand for their products, and they have a business ready to accommodate the sales — but their marketing isn't bringing people in the door and keeping them there. It's inconsistent. There's no structure to it. There is no plan. And even when they think they're checking that marketing box, it rapidly slips right out of their grasp again.

Why? Because Shane, David and Helen are all Technicians.

Michael Gerber coined the term back in 1992, but the principle remains as relevant as ever and these three entrepreneurs are right in the thick of it.

What is a Technician?

Technicians vs Visionaries

The Technician operates in the present and is focused on doing the work of making, troubleshooting and delivering a product. They struggle to grow their business because they're working *in* the business rather than *on* the business day in, day out.

Most people start their business as a Technician. As we've seen, coffee lovers make coffee, mechanics build machinery, property managers serve customers. And they're so overwhelmed with keeping the wheels turning that they don't stop to develop a vision and build the structure needed for their business to thrive.

Unfortunately, Technicians will always struggle to succeed in business. Not because they aren't great at their craft or don't have a great product, but because they haven't built the key foundations their business needs to enable them to move to the Visionary stage.

The Visionary stage is what every business owner craves but rarely achieves. It's the phase when they can walk away from the business and let others run it, with systems in place that automatically find customers, build revenue and weather any storm that comes its way.

When you reach the Visionary stage, you attain true freedom, absolute independence, and total control of your life, your business and your destiny.

So what separates a Technician from a Visionary? What are the steps needed to move from one to the other? And what are so many businesses that ultimately fail every year missing?

The answer is simple: it's called a system.

A system for business operations.

A system for growth.

And, most importantly, a system for your marketing.

If a Technician can let go of their need to do everything, control everyone and manage everybody, they can let the systems take control so they can get on with what they really want to do in life: roasting coffee, making winches or talking about property. They have the choice to do what they want to do, not because they have to, but because they want to.

What would you like to do with your life? How do you want to spend your time? If you want the freedom to step out of the day-to-day running of your business, then you need to embrace a marketing system.

If you want to control your growth, predict your cash flow, build a new product line or go on a five-week holiday, then you need to embrace a marketing system.

As it turns out, I have that system.

This system has been used by over 2000 businesses in the last five years to help them become the Visionary they have always dreamed about.

I have worked with startups, service providers, engineers, consultants, health professionals, technology companies and publicly listed companies.

I have seen them go from being unable to explain their products and services to winning every tender they submit.

I have seen businesses go from struggling to pay their bills to acquiring their competitors.

I have seen owners dishevelled and stressed about their future make marketing decisions with confidence barely six months later.

And it's all because they embraced The Very Good Marketing Framework: a marketing system for small businesses.

So how does The Very Good Marketing Framework work?

Let me demonstrate by showing you how it helped Shane.

The system for success

When I met Shane, it was very clear that he had a great product and was really great at building relationships with customers. But he assumed that great coffee was enough to help him reach his revenue targets. He had a few pieces of a system in place (a website, branding and a product), but was missing a lot of other elements that would enable his business to grow without his constant involvement.

Together, Shane and I rebuilt his entire marketing system using The Very Good Marketing Framework, identifying how to attract new customers, how to convert them, how to onboard them, how to deliver product to them and, finally, how to turn them into his biggest fans. All automatically. Leaving Shane with complete clarity on where he should spend his time, where he should invest his marketing budget and where he is heading in the future.

The Very Good Marketing Framework also helped David who had an amazing way of attracting strangers to his business, but no system for converting them into customers. Together, David and I built a system that would maximise the conversion rate for every viewer of his viral winch video and perpetually grow his leads so he could focus on product development and delivery.

And for Helen, we used The Very Good Marketing Framework to build a system that codified the exact way she grew her business, from how she identified strangers, to how she converted them into customers and how she delivered her products and services so that the method for her success could live on in her company without her.

If you want a marketing system that:

- grows your revenue
- brings new business in with or without your involvement
- makes marketing your business easy

- delivers the kind of success I helped Shane, David and Helen achieve, then The Very Good Marketing Framework is for you.

In this book you will find a step-by-step guide on how to implement this powerful marketing and growth system into your business. Once implemented, you will see a dramatic shift in the way your business operates and how you operate it. You will have more confidence when making decisions and a better chance of reaching your goals, and you can finally start to live the life you've wanted since you started your entrepreneurial journey.

Are there other marketing systems on the market?

You bet. There's the 7Ps Marketing Matrix, Porter's 5 Forces, Acquisition funnels, Pirate Metrics, The Hook Model ... so many marketing models and systems that are inspiring and game changing. They are created by the best minds in the marketing world to accurately predict human behaviour in a consumable market.

'Here is what the customer wants to hear', they'll say.

'Here are seven Ps you need for your business.'

'Three triangles ... '

'A matrix ... '

All slightly different, but all missing one big piece of the puzzle: the how.

How exactly do I use this theory to grow my business? How do I identify this type of customer? How much is it going to cost me? How do I know if it is working? How do I know what to do next?

I love a good marketing framework, but what I love more is a plan to execute it. With a small marketing budget, a small amount of time and a whole lot of risk, a good marketing framework is just not enough for a small business.

If you're lucky, your small business has an $8000 annual budget for marketing and only two hours per week to use it. And whilst you know exactly how to roast coffee, make a winch or manage someone's property, when it comes to spending that marketing budget, you probably don't know where to start.

The reason The Very Good Marketing Framework is so different is because it's practical.

It isn't just a great strategy (it's so much more than that) that's well researched (you bet) and very visual (right-brain thinkers rejoice), it also helps you identify exactly what your next move is. And the move after that, and the move after that, until you have a system in place that operates entirely on its own.

It is so simple and actionable that the likes of Shane, David and Helen have seen it, understood it and used it to drive their business towards their dreams.

It's embedded within hundreds of organisations, it's referenced at university and presented to small-business associations.

It is unbelievably popular because nothing like it exists. And trust me, I've looked. After eight years of supporting small businesses in building websites and executing social media strategies, our agency kept hitting the same roadblocks when it came to giving advice to our small-business clients. There was no framework that was both holistic and practical that we could talk to or hand over or use to give context to the marketing services we were selling.

Most of the clients we worked with were small businesses either growing or starting out. They were (and still are) Technicians looking to live the Australian entrepreneurial dream, who seldom come to the ABN party with a suite of marketing knowledge and technical prowess. So anything we created had to be simple and easy to use.

That's when this marketing framework came to life. It was over four years and with the support of nearly 50 businesses that enabled us to take very complex marketing knowledge, strategies and leading frameworks and create something that has helped so many people reach their goals. It has truly been a collaboration between marketing minds and small business needs as we embedded ourselves within teams and amongst peers to prove that this system works and could continue working for decades to come.

I wrote this book to support as many businesses as I can to become empires, and as many Technicians as I can to become Visionaries. Whether you are just starting out or deep within a growth phase, this book is accessible, simple and easy to implement, and will give you the clarity you need to make decisions about your business with confidence. I've seen too many businesses fail under the weight of poor marketing plans and expensive assets that are not used to their full extent.

But it doesn't have to be yours.

If you want to make confident marketing decisions ...

If you want to eliminate marketing guesswork and wasted money ...

If you want to move from being a Technician to a Visionary ...

This book is for you.

PART I
THERE'S A PROBLEM

Regardless of whether you've been in business for one month or 40 years, the same harsh reality rings true for all of us: running a business is hard.

Really hard.

Couple that with the responsibilities of raising children, caring for loved ones, being in a relationship, and looking after your mental and physical health, running a business on top of that is near impossible. So if you're giving up your time right now to further your business through marketing and to challenge your thinking, then I salute you.

It takes a great deal of effort to step outside of the day to day and commit to the Visionary lifestyle. And you have everything you need to achieve it. There's no question about that.

As your make your way through the first part of this book, I want you to remember that the things that got you here are not going to get you 'there' (i.e. where you want to be). So set aside everything you think you know about marketing and business growth, because in your unknowingness you're going to find the ingredients that grow your business into the vision you've always had for it.

ONE

YOUR MARKETING PLAN IS FAILING AND TAKING YOUR PROFITS WITH IT

No matter how many years your business has been selling to customers, you're probably no closer to unlocking a secret marketing formula than the biggest Fortune 500 companies. Consumer behaviours, communication platforms and a million other external factors mean locking in a 'marketing formula' that stands the test of time is virtually impossible.

Trust me, the ones that lead the way are not in possession of a secret formula; they just have enough cash flow to have top marketers experimenting 24 hours a day, seven days a week to find what works for their business. Most entrepreneurs are lucky to find two hours a month.

If you're familiar with the popular marketing saying, '50 per cent of marketing works; if only we knew which 50 per cent', then you'll know exactly what I am talking about. Trying something new is a risk. It'll cost you a lot of money, it's not guaranteed to work and there are a million avenues to choose from.

Of course, many businesses make it look easy.

And many experts claim to have the 'seven-figure-guaranteed marketing secret' or the '20k per day sales hack' that they used to generate $1 million worth of income with next to no work.

Are these guys for real? Maybe.

Is there really a secret marketing hack? Definitely not.

The promised land

Several years ago, I fell into a bit of a marketing trap that I am almost too embarrassed to admit. It was early 2021 and I was two months away from giving birth to my son. Before this, I was absolutely in denial about going on any kind of maternity leave, but as the date crept closer it was really beginning to sink in that my business-development hat was about to disappear from our company for a while and I needed a quick solution for sustaining our lead flow.

Out of desperation, or possibly just exhaustion, I started a search for a marketing agency dissimilar from our own that could bring in high-value leads for my company while I was on maternity leave. A brand new, cold marketing strategy.

I found an agency in the UK that served me a series of Facebook ads about their secret, proven marketing formula, and I believed they were telling the truth (I should have known better). The first time I met them over a video call late in the evening (because of the time difference), I remember feeling sceptical. They were vague about their special marketing sauce, but fantastic at convincing me it was going to work. I assumed the lack of detail in their proposed strategy was due to the fact we had not signed any contracts yet and I was somewhat of a competitor.

In the weeks to come I was sent a contract and some brief info about a potential campaign, which looked OK. It was the equivalent of AU$10 000 for the campaign set-up and a further $2500 per month for management, plus any advertising spend, which they recommended be between $2000 and $4000.

I signed it.

The first month of the project was labelled as a 'set-up month', which I could only assume involved setting up the campaign copy, and creative and technical elements. They insisted on using a third-party website builder instead of our own website and produced two landing pages using Click Funnels (a funnel building website). It looked OK. I couldn't find the secret formula in it though — it looked straightforward to me. Possibly the secret recipe was in the advertising set-up?

So after four to six weeks of setting up the landing pages, the ad campaign began. I quickly scoured the ads manager to see what was so special about their set-up/creative/wording/imagery.

And much to my absolute disappointment, there was nothing. There was nothing special, nothing out of the ordinary, nothing my team could not have set up themselves. It was Facebook advertising 101.

So, naturally, I panicked. We had just invested $12 500 in a strategy that was not even close to what we would recommend to our clients. It was a disaster. I was embarrassed, and I was out of pocket a lot of money. And, to top it off, at this point I was in hospital on strict bed-rest orders so there wasn't anything I could do even if I wanted to.

I had to let it run its course. Give the campaign some time to deliver some leads. Long story short, I pulled the plug when we hit $20 000 of expenses and no leads. Not one.

The agency was less than cooperative. They wouldn't entertain new ideas on the campaign without us paying more, they didn't seem to have a further strategy beyond what they initially came up with, and they kept claiming that we just needed more time for the campaign to run before we saw results. I felt tricked and taken advantage of and utterly embarrassed.

I have thought a great deal about what transpired in those months over the last few years. It was absolutely one of those pivotal learning experiences that entrepreneurs always reference in their 'journey-to-success' speeches — and not because it sent us broke and brought disaster upon the business, but because it taught us the very lessons that we were trying to teach others. There is no quick marketing hack, no marketing secret, no sudden-millionaire weapon.

If we had stayed on the path with that agency, things may have been different. We would have pivoted the strategy, learnt from the pitfalls, and tried and tested different strategies to bring that campaign to life alongside the other tactics in our business. It would have been a successful long game for us. Not the quick, temporary win I was betting on in my pregnancy-induced, drowsy desperation.

I was drawn in by the money guarantee that never existed. And at some point along your journey, you will be too. Drawn in by the sweet promise of instant success that is so very tempting to an entrepreneur like yourself who carries the weight of everything on their shoulders.

But just like anything in nature, good things take time to grow. Good marketing requires commitment, consistency and, above all else, it requires a considered plan.

At one point, you may have had that plan.

Your business was generating leads and sales and you were hitting the revenue targets you had set out to achieve. The energy you once threw into driving leads to your business lapsed so you could focus on other things: staff things, processing things, product things.

Suddenly, it's six months later, your lead pipeline is hollow, sales are slumping, and you haven't even thought about marketing for months and months. You panic and see the overnight marketing-hack-secret-income-generating-sauce on the internet.

Tempted?

No!

Not you. You're better than this.

There are reasons your marketing plan is failing, and it isn't going to be solved by a quick hack (I am proof of that).

Reason #1: You don't spend time on marketing

Level with me here: how much time do you spend on marketing every week? Every month? Is it something you spend time on consistently or is it sporadic? I bet you don't even have time, am I right?

You have *no* time! Out of all the resources you do have, time is not one of them, and it's very rarely spent working on the business. I would go as far as to say that this is the biggest reason I see growth stop for small businesses. Small-business owners:

◆ don't have any time

◆ don't prioritise it to marketing, and

◆ don't know what to do with it when they do have it.

There's a classic saying in business: 'You need to be thinking about marketing when you don't need it. Because if you wait until you do, it's already too late.'

When you think about this paradox carefully, it likely rings true for your own business. Product-buying cycles for customers are such that if you wait until you have the time, until your business is quiet, until you have a dire need to market to them, there just won't be enough time to generate the momentum you need to survive. So, depending on what industry you're in, your lack of time could be catastrophic.

I work with a lot of clients that are in the B2B (business to business) space. To be more specific, this next example is in the B2BB (business to big-business service) — something I just made up to emphasis the exceptionally long buying cycles that come with selling product to big business, with their big budgets but also their big bureaucracy and multiple approvals that need to take place before a quote is approved.

One client of ours delivers leadership development services to big business. Her business services are demanded at different times of the year, but usually line up to things like National Safe Work Month or the end of the financial year when budgets need to be spent.

Throughout the rest of the year, she is fairly quiet.

So, for her, April to July is packed with work and so is September to November (with October being National Safe Work Month).

Her average buying cycle is six months, which means that for her business to run effectively, she needs to be undertaking marketing *and* doing all her product delivery in the same months.

It's chaos.

When she reflects on this, she laughs. She says, 'It's the unluckiest of flukes, that when I have the least amount of time all year, I must make the time for marketing and sales. These are the times we are supposed to be focusing on our service delivery and, instead, we are working on getting the next job.'

The kicker is if she didn't, she wouldn't survive.

Making time for marketing and sales is the biggest, most important thing you can do if you want to reach your goals. One of our biggest fears, though, is giving up that time for marketing and not using it on something that seems more important or more urgent.

Those emails from those customers?

That interview?

Sorting out that quality problem?

All very important. But what is prioritising them costing you?

'You don't need more time. You just need to use the time you have better.'

I carry this quote with me everywhere. We are all given 24 hours in a day. Whether you want to grow your business, spend time with loved ones, pick up a new hobby, work on your fitness — whatever is important to you deserves time. And you can't make time, you must trade for time.

Don't lose sight of what is important versus what is urgent in your business. You need to make time for things like marketing. (Forget about *what* to do with that time. I'll tell you what to do later.)

I guarantee you that the more time you, the founder, dedicate to the marketing of your business, the more leads, customers and fans you will generate. Almost exponentially.

But, for now, let's just start small.

Go get your calendar out and block out some non-negotiable time each week to work *on* the business, not *in* the business. For my company it's Tuesdays. We call it 'hours of power'. We all get three hours from 8:30am to 11:30am to work together on marketing our business, and using our technical expertise to overcome any of our marketing bottlenecks.

Allocating and dedicating the time is the very first step. Just like any investment, time is a precious resource that can repay ten-fold. Allocating this time is going to be the number one thing you can do to ensure your future is different to your present.

Reason #2: You aren't focused

So it's 8.30 am Tuesday morning and you're ready for your 'hours of power'. You've got your coffee ready, your inbox is closed, your 'do not disturb' has been set on your phone, and you're ready to 'do marketing'.

So what do you do?

Lack of focus is a really big problem that small-business owners face. Not just in marketing, but in every business discipline. When there's a thousand competing priorities, it can seem impossible to give just one thing all of your attention. The result is that nothing gets completed — or worse, completed to terrible standards.

In the words of Gary Keller, author of *The One Thing*, 'In your effort to attend to all things, everything gets short changed and nothing is done.'

Marketing is the same. There are not only hundreds of options available to you and your business, but hundreds of ways to execute each marketing method — and no limits around them.

What I mean by that is that any other business task is finite. If you have to complete a Business Activity Statement (BAS), the task is complete when you submit the BAS. The actions involved to complete it are always the same, the outcome is always the same. There is one path.

When it comes to marketing, tasks are never straightforward. Marketing is variable, it is ongoing, and the frequency and nature of tasks are so different every time that it makes creating a static marketing plan and checklist very hard. It also makes sitting down and 'doing marketing' quite an unsettling task if you aren't sure what to focus on.

I was in a meeting with my team the other day, and we were talking about all the actions we were working on for a client project leading up to a new product launch. I could feel the overwhelm in the room. There was a lot that needed to be done.

At the end of the meeting, I asked the team what they thought was the number one thing on the list right now? What was the most important thing?

One by one, everyone said something different.

We lacked focus because there were so many things that seemed equally important and could each lead to the best outcome. And our disparity was not going to lead to the best outcome for the client.

What I've found, time and time again, is that when it comes to marketing, businesses spread themselves thin. Really thin, across everything.

Ask a business owner what they are doing exceptionally well, and it's not a lot of things.

Ask them what's in progress, and there's a lot.

When you spread yourself thin, it takes a very long time for anything to reach its maturity. And that's why a lot of small businesses fail. Nothing quite gets finished, or nothing quite gets to 100 per cent of what it could.

So, we have a bit of a saying to remedy this: Do it 105 per cent or not at all.

This idea is going to come up again later in the book because it is very important. It is going to help you decide what marketing methods to choose for your business and commit to them.

Focus on one thing, give it 105 per cent and it will do so much more for your business than 50 things you're giving 2 per cent of effort to a day.

In marketing we see a lot of 2 per centers.

It's the social media page that hasn't been used for eight months.

It's the Google Business listing that is out of date.

It's the About Us page on the website with team members who no longer work there.

It's a customer service email that gets responded to six days late.

It's 'I'll get to it eventually', rather than, 'this is my number one priority'.

Perhaps it's inattention to where the focus needs to be directed.

Or it's the perceived risk of focusing on one thing to the exclusion of all others.

But no matter what the reason, a lack of focus is one of the top reasons your marketing is failing.

Reason #3: You don't have a system

Michael E Gerber is one of the world's best business authors. He's nearly 90 now, and his book *The E-Myth Revisited: Why most small businesses don't work and what to do about it* is possibly one of the most cited books for small-to-medium enterprises (SMEs) to date.

Now, there are plenty of books out there written for SMEs, but none have stuck like the fable in Gerber's book. He is responsible for transforming thousands of businesses over the last few decades just through the simple idea of systemising your business.

'Let systems run the business, and people run the systems', he says.

So many SMEs don't have any systems within their business. Even systems as simple as the process to manufacture your products or the process in answering the phone.

Raising a quote.

Invoicing a client.

When you can systemise your business, you can do things like franchise it or double it in size or sell it. And it is separate from you as the business owner.

The way you generate business for your business needs to be its own system, and it is an important one.

'How are we expected to write down how we do sales? It's different every time', said Ron, sales agent for an international battery technology company.

Ron is based in Turkey and is the sales agent for the western Asian region. He is very good at his job, and doesn't particularly like being questioned about how he does it.

'I agree with Ron', Dan chimed in on the videoconference. Dan was in Amsterdam, as the sales agent for northern Europe. He didn't really see how Ron's process had anything to do with his process in Europe — they were completely different.

In fact, amongst all eight international sales agents in the meeting, none of them were that keen on taking the time to document exactly how they did their job. It made it easier for the company to replace them, surely. Or worse — tell them how to do their job.

'Our sales numbers aren't where we want them to be', said the general manager back at Australian headquarters. 'Our CRM indicates the volume of leads is steady, but sales numbers just aren't improving like we want.'

This had been the trend for the last 12 months for this technology company. When I met with them back in 2020 to discuss their marketing, and they couldn't produce a codified sales or marketing system, their first task was to find out what was being done out in the field.

Except nobody could tell them.

How was the company supposed to improve something that didn't exist? (How are you?)

Systems were a big part of how this company manufactured its product, so the idea of a process wasn't new to them. It was just a bit of a challenge to convince their team that marketing and sales should be captured as a system as well.

'Every time, it depends on the product, the customer, the stage of their project, the budget', Ron rambled on. 'It's not possible', he concluded.

Finally, when it was my turn to talk, I explained the task: 'If something isn't working, you need to know what it is as soon as possible. The only way you can do that is by knowing what is being done, and if something different is being done every time, it's virtually impossible to make conclusions and remedy it.'

It took some time, but eventually the team developed a high-level sales process that included when/how to introduce brochures, unique selling points, case studies and discounts. The entire process enabled the different agents to share stories and learnings, and work with the marketing team to create things that would further enhance their process.

Notwithstanding the benefits of a formal system, the act of sharing knowledge capital amongst individuals around the world was one of the single most impactful things this company did to shift their conversion rate. And the habit of reviewing the system and collaborating ensured new agents were able to hit the ground running with success as they grew.

Reason #4: You don't do data

If your marketing plan is failing, it is likely because you aren't using the right marketing and sales numbers to make decisions. This one is two-fold because when I say the 'right' marketing and sales numbers, I am alluding to the reality that data nowadays seems to be either in over-abundance or not present at all.

Many businesses are flush with data. It is coming out of their ears, and a lot of it just doesn't make sense — especially digital data that comes from website management or ad campaigns.

On the other side of that is the complete absence of data. No sales data, no conversion rates, no knowledge about lifetime customers and fans. Just an empty guess.

The result of both realities is that data often gets neglected altogether because finding the right data is just too damn hard.

You've likely heard of the famous quote by Peter Drucker: 'What gets measured gets managed.' The basic tenet is that if you're measuring something like marketing or sales, then the probability of you using that information for decision-making (and, therefore, success) is a lot higher.

So, if data is something you aren't collecting or using, it could be the reason that your marketing is failing you. If you can't see where you are succeeding or failing with cold, hard numbers, then you are wasting precious marketing money.

Reason #5: Your relationship with marketing experts is bad

As a small-business owner or leader, it is likely you will not have all the resources available to execute all of your own marketing tasks from scratch. Whether that is graphic design work, advertising, website development, photography, social media etc., there will have been a point in your journey when an agency, freelancer or consultant was engaged.

If you are relying on a marketing expert now to implement your marketing activities for you, chances are that relationship could be better. And it needs to be if you are going to get the most out of their professional experience.

I can relay hundreds of conversations I have had about unhealthy relationships between agencies and small-business owners. So many stories of misunderstood briefs or financial abuse — I even witnessed one instance where an SME owner had to conduct their own investigation to discover that the forwarding number for their Google Ads account was incorrect.

These issues come up time and time again (heck, I was even victim to a bit of agency misalignment), so it is important to understand why it keeps happening and how you can make the most of your marketing-expert-to-business relationship.

Importantly, not all marketing-expert-to-business relationships are poor. The best ones are built on mutual understanding of the business strengths, realistic outcomes and communication — for both parties.

We used to work with a client whose view of her business strengths, desired outcomes and communication expectations differed vastly from ours. Where most clients would fit into a once- or twice-monthly communication rhythm, this client would call me every week — multiple times. Text, WhatsApp, everything. The communication expectation was not clear, and it did not lead to the best outcome for either of us. To make matters worse, every call she made to us used up her marketing budget as our team would be clocking time to her business. This left very little time for actual 'marketing work', which didn't produce the outcomes she wanted and made the relationship very tense.

As she was the owner of a beauty salon, the way I contextualised it for her was to compare the behaviour to me coming into her salon sporadically over a couple of weeks to have a few eyebrow hairs plucked and then expecting to pay the same appointment fee when I arrive for my full shaping appointment.

Whilst not all marketing agencies have rules around communication (and not all salons have rules about sporadic eyebrow-hair pop-ins), it was essential that we got on the same page about things like communication to get the best results.

COMMUNICATION

So start by locking in how often you going to communicate. Who will you be communicating with? What is your expectation for communication and what is theirs? Getting on top of these things is important for success. Remember that communication takes time, and when it comes to a service like marketing, time is the commodity. So, the more time you spend communicating, the more this is going to cost your business. Ensure you are on the same page with your marketing company about how much this time costs, what is included and how much you receive in your quote.

Similar to how you communicate is the language you are communicating with. Marketing lingo (which can manifest in abbreviations, technical terms and insider phrases) can often leave business owners feeling a little lost. Follow up on lingo you don't understand so that you increase your knowledge and can have better conversations about strategy, rather than feeling overwhelmed. This is essential to combining their skills with your intimate understanding of your business for the best outcome.

BUSINESS STRENGTHS

Ensure you have ample time together to communicate your business strengths to each other. They need to understand yours, but also take the time to understand theirs, so you feel comfortable with their marketing strategy.

Sometimes working with a marketing company is a bit like a gossip chain where the message you relay to one person has to trickle down and down until the creative that assembles it only has a loose understanding of what your business does and what you are looking to achieve. How can you rectify this? Can it be relayed in a document, video or notes so the whole team is across it?

REALISTIC OUTCOMES

Goal setting every year, or every quarter, is absolutely essential to ensure you and your marketing provider are both on the same trajectory. They will be able to give you realistic feedback on what is possible for your budget/business/resources, and you can hold them accountable to those results.

This process is essential not just for improving your agency-business relationship, but as an integral part of shaping your entire marketing strategy. As we work through the chapters in this book, it is important to quantify your goals and your budget and resources so you can bridge that gap between your present state and your future goals effectively.

Reason #6: Your marketing foundations aren't strong

So, remember our friend David whose YouTube video went viral?

David had the start of an amazing business. He had an awesome product and he had customers who were dying to buy it. What he didn't have was the rest of his marketing and sales foundations in place to sustain a sudden influx of strangers wanting his product.

And this is where I see so many businesses slip up.

A lot of businesses have a marketing strategy in some form, whether that is part of their business plan or based on a theoretical model. (Luckily, David had a great website 😊) But for a lot of other businesses, all their good work attracting strangers, doing networking and getting good word of mouth might be wasted because their website isn't converting visitors into proper leads.

And to that end, many businesses don't have a mechanism for converting leads into customers effectively, or else they lose those customers before they have a chance to become real fans. Every interaction a customer has with your business must be carefully considered. It doesn't even have to be perfect; it just needs to be something.

An accounting company we began work with recently invited me to come out and meet with their two founders, Ben and Sarah. The pair were young and enthusiastic, and clearly passionate about the SMEs they helped.

They openly told me they didn't need marketing. All their business came from word of mouth, so they didn't need a website or a social media profile.

The pair had built quite a thriving business over the last few years through strong word of mouth and (clearly) amazing customer service. They grew their team from seven people to 30 in just over three years, and without any 'marketing' help whatsoever.

They told me their philosophy to growth was 'good work for their current customers', and that alone was the key to bringing in new business.

Except for lately. Lately they weren't generating any new customers at all, not for three to six months. Ergo, my attendance.

'So, you don't have a website at all?' I asked over coffee.

'Nope.'

'So, when one of your customers refers you to a friend, where do they go to learn more about you?'

'They call us', Ben said.

'Of course', I agreed. 'But maybe we should look at setting up an online presence. A website, a Google Business listing? You could be getting 100 referrals a month, but they can't find you online, so they think you're not legit.'

Both founders looked a bit taken aback by that.

'If someone recommended a lawyer to you, for example, would you go see them if they didn't have any kind of online presence? Or a home builder? We're talking about people's money. It's a big deal and a decision they won't take lightly. They're going to do due diligence.'

After a while, they both agreed. They needed some foundations in place so they could continue compounding their word of mouth over time as their major marketing tool.

Reason #7: You've got a leaky bucket

So, imagine you have some foundations in place, and you feel OK about your marketing so far, but you still aren't reaching your goals. What isn't working?

The seventh and final reason marketing fails for SMEs is the leaky bucket. And what I mean by that is the water (or the customers) escaping through holes in the bucket (your marketing strategy) you didn't even realise were there.

When you're investing in marketing to strangers, you are pouring water in the top of this bucket you assume is completely sturdy. You have a website, you have a sales team, you have a great product.

But over time, you realise that bucket isn't sturdy at all.

Your sales team is inundated; they take days to reply to enquiries.

Your website doesn't have a call-to-action button.

Your competitors have products that have overtaken yours.

Without realising it, all the water you have paid good money acquiring has escaped when it shouldn't have.

SKIRTING THE SALE

My team moved into a new office over a year ago. The office we absolutely loved and made our home for three years was sold and our lease was not renewed. But we found a new office, just around the corner with arguably better views, plus it was much closer to the coffee, so things were not all bad.

When we moved in we had to update some of the electrical work and the skirting boards had to be temporarily removed from a few walls to make it happen. A year later, we still hadn't replaced the skirting boards.

Resist rolling your eyes at us! We just hadn't gotten around to it.

Anyway, three months ago, I found the matching skirting boards and emailed the company for a quote. Weeks passed and I had still not received the quote. So, I followed up with the company and received this reply.

'Hello Amy, I sent the quote two weeks ago. Here is a screenshot with proof I sent it. You must not have checked. Are you proceeding with the quote? Amanda'

I replied, 'Thanks for sending it through, Amanda. I am happy to proceed with the quote.'

A few months passed, and I received another email.

'Hello Amy, have you had a chance to review our quote? Can you tell me when you require the skirting for your project? Could we please have an update on this project's current status? ANY feedback is useful to us and valued. Amanda'

So, I replied, 'Amanda, I am happy to proceed with the quote, and it would be great if installation can happen fairly quickly. Do you have an estimated date that it can be installed?'

A few weeks later I received another reply, 'Hello Amy, thanks for getting back to me. At this stage we are fully booked for the remainder of the year. Can you let me know when you plan to complete this trade? We need a mark-up plan of the office. Amanda'

To which I replied, 'We need this work done as soon as possible, so please let me know when the earliest time that it can be done is. It would be great if someone could come out and have a look at the space or let me know what drawings you require.'

And to this date, I have not received a reply, and we still don't have skirting boards.

Now don't get me wrong, I should have asked for another quote from another company, but I was holding out for Amanda to come around. And the skirting boards her company supplied were an exact match.

It's likely that what was happening to me was possibly happening to other leads wanting to become a customer. And I would bet that if the owner of the company were aware, they would be mortified. Little holes like this in an otherwise solid bucket are one of the reasons marketing is failing SMEs.

When your business is growing rapidly, when you are not involved in the day to day anymore, things like this get missed.

And the impact could be catastrophic.

HAD A BAD DAY

Georgia was a team member who worked for Helen's property management company in North Perth. She spent her days at work fielding phone calls from tenants and property owners regarding the day-to-day running of several residential properties across the city.

Some days were good: minimal complaints to field, easy questions, good weather.

Some days her first phone call was a disgruntled tenant, calling for the fifth time in the peak of summer demanding the air-conditioning in the property be fixed immediately. 'I'll pass this onto the owner again', she would say.

'Just *fix it,* otherwise, I am coming down there personally to find you and make you fix it', the tenant would yell and hang up the phone.

Understandably, Georgia was disheartened, and her customer service demeanour for the rest of the day was affected. Georgia was a member of an eight-person team, all fielding phone calls like this every day.

So, when it came to the meeting I had with them, it was not really a surprise that they had a serious customer churn rate. Not only were they not converting a lot of current customers into fans, but a lot of them were actually leaving their business altogether, meaning that their marketing needed to provide them with enough new visitors, leads and customers to help them grow, and also to replace the ones they had already lost.

It was quite a big challenge.

For this company, converting customers to fans was their biggest bottleneck, and it is quite a common bottleneck for many service-based businesses (more on this in chapter 3).

Team having a good day? You got amazing service.

Team having a bad day? You feel like you've been short changed.

The most important thing a business can do is ensure they are delivering their products and services the same way every time before they even look at improving their conversion rate from customers to fans.

Is there a way of overcoming all these problems and creating a marketing strategy that gives you visibility into leaks and helps you build foundations whilst also giving you time and data? Yes.

Is it in this book? *Yes.*

Is it really complicated? *No.*

You must be kidding me? *I am not.*

I meet so many people on different stages of their business growth. And one of the big differences between them isn't so much their actions as it is their ongoing mindset.

We build a cognitive bias towards taking actions that are familiar to us.

Have you ever wondered why some people are so easy to coach and some people never take action at all? A lot of the time it is because making change is hard and going against something we already made our mind up about is near impossible. When it comes to making decisions about marketing, some ideas or biases are going to be hard to let go.

Top ten myths about SME marketing

Understandably, everything I have said so far may seem too good to be true. So let me bust a few myths about marketing to make sure you have confidence in the process we are about to undertake.

Myth 1: Marketing is constantly changing; there's no way I can keep up

It is true that marketing as an industry and a practice has changed quite a lot over the last few decades. It transforms as technology transforms, and many of the channels we once used to broadcast our messages or build relationships with consumers have become obsolete or morphed completely.

However, the speed at which they change is not as fast as you may think. Yes, it is fast if you only tune into marketing once a year, but maintaining a weekly cadence for popping your head into the world of marketing ensures you are keeping on top of what is going on so that you can understand (at least at a high level) where your consumers are spending time and how to reach them.

Myth 2: There's a secret trick to marketing

As I personally, painstakingly discovered, there is no secret trick to good marketing. There are best practices, there are proven techniques and there are amazing things that happen with time and consistency, but there is no magic, secret formula. All good things take time, and just as it is for goals like saving money, losing weight or learning a skill, small and deliberate actions towards success will always compound into something great.

Myth 3: I need a formal education to be good at it

There is no formal education in marketing that is guaranteed to give business owners a unique advantage in marketing their business. The learning you will receive from reading articles and books (like this one) or just taking the time to ask the experts the right questions will do just as much as a formal education in today's world.

Some education may help you deep dive into particular marketing technology; however, what will really help you as a business owner is grasping a high-level strategy for your business that enables you to pick and choose areas your business will benefit from. Only then can you implement the right marketing for your business, whether that be through outsourcing or targeted learning opportunities.

Myth 4: Marketing is expensive

Yes, it is true that marketing can be expensive; however, not all marketing activities (especially the ones in this book) come at a cost. A lot of them are completely free to implement and a lot of them can be done yourself. Good marketing advice can be expensive, but it can also be free. It is often a case of working through your marketing system and identifying *where* to spend your budget, not *what* your budget needs to be in order to succeed.

Myth 5: I need to outsource all of it

False. Yes, marketing can seem overwhelming and confusing, but it really isn't so complex. This marketing guide is going to make it easy for you to grasp, and then when you want to implement something, you can decide whether you want to upskill to learn how to do it or outsource it. You have the choice, and you need to be in control.

Myth 6: I need to keep all of it in house

Also false. The key, again, is to be in control of the marketing strategy as the owner of the business, and then use internal or external tools to bring the strategy to life. With the right communication with any external contractors, you can get the results you want without having to pay for someone in-house.

Myth 7: My competitors know something I don't

It is easy to see someone else's success and think that they are worlds ahead of you in terms of knowledge or results. The truth is that your competitors are likely sitting on the same information you are, and are grappling with the same decision-making fatigue when it comes to marketing. You only have two options when it comes to your competitors. The first is to ignore them completely; focus on what you are doing 105 per cent. The second is to watch what they are doing and learn from their successes or failures. Learn from their 105 per cent.

Myth 8: My competitors are spending more money on marketing than me

This is often a myth as well. If a competitor is giving something 105 per cent effort where you have only been able to manage 5 per cent, it can seem impossible to fathom how they are executing it. As you will discover, once you start giving something 105 per cent effort consistently, it becomes easier and easier to manage, which may be the case for your competitors.

Similarly, if you have engaged with their business like a consumer would, for example, by visiting their website, they may be targeting (or following) you with digital advertisements. It may seem like they are everywhere and spending big, but in fact, you are the only one seeing it.

Myth 9: Any DIY marketing efforts I make are going to be terrible

Let me paint a picture for you of this one. Imagine you had 2.5 hours per week to focus on marketing. You had absolutely no marketing currently running, and you picked up this book to start from scratch.

With 2.5 hours a week, only one bottleneck to beat (we will get into this soon) and nothing else to distract you, it is going to be easy to get good at the DIY marketing task that you are implementing. The majority of your competitors are either doing nothing at all or tackling marketing with much less effort and deliberation than you are. So give yourself some confidence! You will have time, focus and consistency behind you this time, and your efforts will be way better than you think.

Myth 10: A strategy is the same as a plan

Semantics may trip you up on this one, but following The Very Good Marketing Framework helps you create a strategy for your business. It is the guiding star that is going to help you focus and use your budget effectively. Choosing the tasks you implement on your journey toward that guiding star is the plan.

Many businesses create a plan with steps without a guiding strategy to shape those tasks. When they look back, they find they're actually not being led by anything at all, and those tasks aren't coming together to create something amazing. Plans need to be fluid and tasks may be responsive, but as long as you are being guided by something concrete, proven and deliberate (such as this guide), you will never be off track.

TWO

THE VERY GOOD MARKETING FRAMEWORK

When I was working as a consultant, I was having a lot of the same conversations with business owners.

'You have a website, but how are people going to find it?'

'You're using social media, but how do you know if it's working?'

'Your customers love you, but how are you using them to grow your business further?'

The further we delved into discussions like this, the broader and more complex marketing became, and I could do very little to consolidate marketing into something digestible for business owners to grow their business. The more I shed light on what was essential or required to cover off under 'marketing', the more concerned looks I received, and the more I could sense sighs and dread around budgets and time and effort.

Perhaps this has been your experience with marketing too? As soon as you tackle one thing, it doesn't seem to be enough. So you look at something else, which opens up different options, and suddenly you're looking at the hundreds of marketing channels out there wondering exactly what is next for your business. It's exhausting and it's overwhelming.

But it doesn't have to be like that. And so many businesses that have crossed over from a small to a medium business and even large business have sat in your place now, wondering just how they can finally get a grip on the craft that is marketing.

When I began my search for marketing frameworks and tools that would help, it seemed even more confusing. There was nothing holistic or simple enough to support small-business owners to really get a grip on their entire marketing system in a way that gave them value and clarity, rather than overwhelm or confusion.

The Very Good Marketing Framework is the culmination of four years of research, hundreds of willing participants and thousands of customers. It is a systems-thinking model that visually depicts the linear customer journey from stranger to fan in a way that pinpoints exactly where a small business needs to spend their marketing budget to reach their goals *and* continue improving their performance for years to come. It isn't a 'secret marketing hack', but it sure is a game changer, and I've never met a case it doesn't work for. Let me tell you more about it ...

The five Cs of Very Good Marketing

The Very Good Marketing Framework contains one visual model, five commitments and a Very Simple Principle. Before we dive into the model, it is important that you commit to the five Cs of Very Good Marketing. They are the guiding commitments that are the difference between the businesses that fail and the ones that succeed. When I look back at all the conversations I've had with buried businesses about their marketing, the common ingredients that were missing are the same ones that made others fly: clarity, consistency, commitment, communication and constant improvement.

Chances are when it comes to your marketing, at least one — if not all five — of these are letting you down and holding you back from reaching your goals.

1. Clarity

If you do not have clarity on where you want to get to and the steps required to get you there, you'll likely never make it. In business, there are many moving parts across many disciplines, and it is very hard to have clarity around everything. However, it is not impossible. And when it comes to marketing, having clarity around the high-level strategy that is going to help you reach your goals is essential.

Human beings naturally turn away from confusion and toward clarity. Clarity helps us understand and make sense of the world around us. When things are clear and concise, we are able to more easily process and retain information, which can help us make better decisions and solve problems more effectively.

Think of clarity as the choice between a map handed to you at the start of a hedge maze and going in alone. Eventually, you will get to where you want to get to (I hope), but with the map providing clarity around your path, your steps and your goal, you are going to make it there more efficiently and quickly.

Clarity is built into every step of implementing The Very Good Marketing Framework, and with clarity around your current position, your next steps and your future state, there'll be nothing cloudy about it.

2. Consistency

Consistency in business is everything. It's in how you manufacture products, how you complete tasks, how you guarantee safety and how you build efficiencies. So many parts of your marketing system probably lack consistency, especially when it comes to those tasks managed by individuals.

If your customer doesn't experience a consistent journey from when they are a stranger to your business, through to when they are a customer, then they will seldom make it all the way through to becoming your biggest fan because their journey has had too many ups and downs.

My favourite fable to demonstrate consistency and how easy it is to ignore in a marketing context is that of the man in a barber shop.

THE BEST HAIRCUT HE'S EVER HAD

A man walks into a quiet barbershop on a busy city lane, late in the afternoon. As he steps over the threshold and inside the small shop, he is quickly greeted by a warm, friendly assistant who invites him to sit down in an empty barber's chair.

The man is immediately offered his choice of beverage. He chooses a beer, and to his surprise, the assistant brings him one. It is cold and refreshing. The assistant asks the man whether he would like to watch something on the TV. 'Why not?' the man exclaims.

Once he has settled into watching a live sports game with his cold beer, the barber comes over to introduce himself and asks the man how he would like his hair cut. 'Just nice and neat, please', the man tells him.

Over the next 20 minutes, the barber cuts his hair, invites him to pay with a smile and then moves on to the next customer. Upon inspection in the window of the shop as he leaves, he thinks to himself, smiling, 'This was the best haircut I've ever had.'

The next time he needs another trim, the man is excited to return to his new favourite barbershop.

He travels down the city lane to arrive at the quiet shop ready for a great haircut, a cold beer and a bit of TV. When he crosses the threshold into the barbershop, the assistant who greeted him last time is busy with another customer. So he stands awkwardly in the entrance, unsure whether to go in and take a seat or just stay put.

Eventually, the assistant comes over and invites him to sit down in an empty barber's chair and walks away. No beer and no TV are offered. After ten minutes, the barber comes over and greets the man politely to begin his haircut.

Upon leaving the store, the man catches his reflection in the window again and thinks, 'Yeah, it's still the best haircut I've ever had.'

Weeks later, when the man requires yet another haircut, he makes the same journey down the city lane to the quiet barbershop. However, this time, when he crosses the threshold of the store, there is nobody there but the barber and his current customer. Again, he lingers in the entrance waiting for someone to greet him and instruct him where to sit. After 20 minutes of waiting, the barber finishes up with his current customer, helps him pay and then ushers the man into the same seat as his previous patron. It's warm and he can feel the tickle of freshly cut hair against his back as he leans against the chair.

After a 20-minute haircut, he pays the barber and leaves the shop. Catching himself in the window he thinks, 'This is still a great haircut.' But he won't return.

It's not for the lack of a great haircut (it was a great haircut), but because once he'd received that amazing service the first time, and then had it taken away from him, all subsequent trips were a disappointment.

This story is a textbook example of the importance of consistency, and how it is just as important to be consistent as it is to offer any service at all. As a consumer, we expect consistency when it comes to the goods and services that we repeatedly pay for. We want the branding, customer service and product performance to be the same across our whole journey. In some ways, we acknowledge this at the time; for example, 'This coffee is always great.' At other times, our need for consistency only manifests itself in times of inconsistency; for example, 'My online order arrived later than it usually would' or 'That sales assistant was rude.'

If your experiences with a company start to vary, your commitment and loyalty to them falters, because suddenly there is a risk that the product, service or experience might not be adequate.

Conversely, if you know what to expect, you will be more likely to return.

3. Commitment

For your marketing to reach its full potential, you must be willing to embrace new and different ideas, and regard growth as the realisation of successful experiments. Hard experience taught me that marketing success is unpredictable. One day we are certain the way to market a luxury product is through magazines and billboards, the next we are putting our marketing in the hands of local or micro social media influencers. Most of the time marketing is just a series of educated guesses and risks, with no right answer and not much predictability behind it. You need to embrace that, and the paradox is that you will always grow faster if you are willing to commit to experiments, accept the outcome and move forward.

The best bit is that the more experiments you run, the sooner you will find your optimal strategy. Most businesses will stick to what is common and safe, or else let the loudest and most convincing voice guide their marketing decisions. This approach will only get you caught up in the noise of your competitors. Every experiment you run is going to teach you more about your customers, your company and the way you have articulated your products. Experimenting will give you the clarity you need to adjust things going forward.

Experiments do not always have to be risky. In chapter 4, we are going to talk about running risk-averse marketing experiments and how to do them in a way that fosters divergent thinking. The key is to commit to each experiment 105 per cent with a target in mind. If that experiment does not hit the target, you should move on to the next experiment. If it does hit that target, you should keep it running and then move onto another experiment.

Often, I see businesses running multiple experiments at once, dabbling in a hot marketing trend and giving multiple projects 5 per cent or 10 per cent of effort. If you cannot guarantee that you have put 105 per cent effort into that one channel, then you will never know for sure whether it is your optimal strategy or not. Most businesses have little marketing success because they don't commit to experiments that unlock their ultimate strategy — not because they don't have a good product offering.

The good news for you is that your product offering has got you this far. It is already good, and you just need to find the marketing strategy that works for you.

4. Communication

Regardless of whether your organisation has three or 300 people, you will find that the greatest success lies in your ability to communicate your marketing strategy to all stakeholders, whether they are people within your business or the marketing supports you hire around your business to help you bring your strategy to life.

When communication is clear and transparent, it helps to build trust and improve collaboration, which can be particularly important in stakeholder relationships essential to marketing success, such as those with internal team members and external professionals. Many organisations miss out on crucial growth because individuals inside their business aren't aware of how their day-to-day role positively or negatively affects a wider strategy.

A scary picture painted by Harvard Business School claims that only 7 per cent of employees understand what their company's growth strategy is and how their role contributes to it. Some employees in the study claimed to know what the company objectives were, but they seldom understood how they related to their day-to-day tasks.

Collective and organisation-wide transparency of your marketing and growth strategy fosters new creative ideas and improves performance. It will empower each person in your organisation to take responsibility for their own contribution to success and provide them with clear, meaningful and manageable numbers for which they can be accountable on a regular basis.

5. Constant improvement

I have seen many set-and-forget marketing plans. They are very easy to spot. They can be seen in the Google Ads campaign that runs the same ads month after month without attempting to improve conversions. In the website that is updated once a decade with no news, no blog and no indication that the business is actually in business. Or in the Facebook page with no updates in eight months. Basically, they are 'marketing-is-an-afterthought' plans that are taking those businesses to another flatline year.

In today's marketing world, you must be present, you have to pay attention and you have to run experiments and work hard to reach the goals you have set. You can't simply come up with an idea and then set and forget it. Your marketing strategy needs deliberate attention. You should never shift your focus away from improving and creating the future you envision.

If you practice constant improvement, you can distil your actions into the simple approach of believing everything can do better. Every touchpoint across your customer journey can be improved, even by 1 per cent, and when you can clearly see how those touchpoints are influencing the overall marketing system, you can work systematically to improve them, rather than setting up a marketing plan and then looking at reactive metrics 12 months later.

Committing to the five Cs is the best way to change your future trajectory. The five Cs can be found in the marketing and business strategy of every SME success story, and they need to be part of yours too. Without them at the forefront of your marketing strategy, any other changes are futile. When I've attempted to implement the visual model of this framework into businesses that haven't committed to the 5Cs, the results are never as permanent or as powerful.

The Very Good Marketing Model

How fantastic would it be if every stranger in your target market woke up tomorrow morning with the sudden urge to buy your product. And a moment later, had purchased. Just like that.

Wouldn't that be nice.

But let's be honest, it's never going to happen like that.

What happens is that a stranger goes through quite a journey before they buy from you, and a bit of a journey afterwards as well.

The journey your customer takes from being a stranger to a customer and beyond is known as the customer journey. Many marketing theorists have documented parts of this journey, and the way a customer interacts with and understands your company along the way. But my version is much simpler. And you don't need to understand marketing at all to make sense of it.

So let me introduce to you to The Very Good Marketing Model.

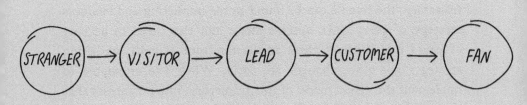

The Very Good Marketing Model is the linear journey that your customer goes through from being a stranger all the way through to becoming your biggest fan. Because it is a linear journey (a customer doesn't wake up and purchase from you without going through these steps), it is easy to see where the journey or the system breaks down. You can attribute any marketing method to a stage the customer is currently on, and very quickly see what the purpose of every activity is.

Let's go through exactly what each stage means.

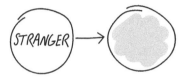

The Stranger

As the name implies, a customer journey starts with someone who doesn't know you at all. They are a complete stranger to your business, and your products or services solve a problem they have.

This is a really important stage of your customer journey to identify, because the primary purpose of most marketing channels that are thrown around (e.g. search engine optimisation (SEO), search engine marketing (SEM), social ads) is to attract Strangers to your business and turn them into Visitors. Nobody miraculously knows your website URL; they have had to be told about it somewhere.

Which leads me to the next stage of your customer journey.

The Visitor

A Visitor is someone who has been introduced to your company and then visited it. They either visited your website, your store or your social media page to learn more about you.

They are no longer a Stranger to your business, but they are not quite having a two-way conversation with you; they are passively collecting information.

Lots of marketing professionals and strategies focus on turning Strangers into Visitors and then stop the journey there. However, Visitors are worthless to your business unless they take the next step in the journey and become a Lead.

The Lead

A Lead is a pretty integral part of your business and a turning point on any customer journey. It's the point when a Stranger makes contact with your business and begins a two-way conversation with you (e.g. you can contact them; they can contact you).

When someone is a Lead, you have more opportunity to try and convince them to become a Customer by understanding their individual needs. Again, many marketing theories and marketing services stop here. Lead has been delivered. Job done.

However, I meet more businesses struggling to take their Leads on the rest of the customer journey than any other area of marketing, including becoming the Customer.

The Customer

Hello Customers, it is you we have been looking for!

You are why we exist. And we can't exist without you.

Make no mistake, Customers are seen most often as the end game of marketing, and they're probably the most important number that businesses will reflect and report on.

But what if there is more?

What if the Customer is not the end of the journey?

Would it surprise you to know there is one more incredibly important part?

Stopping at the Customer stage is a fool's game. The real pot of gold at the end of your customer journey is the Fan.

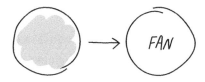

The Fan

Glorious Fan, you are worth so much more than any marketer realises.

A Fan is worth ten times what one Customer is worth.

They are so important because they are the ones who become advocates for your business. They buy from you again and again, they tell friends about you, and they provide you with the reviews and testimonials that convert Strangers.

It costs upwards of five to six times as much to turn a Stranger into a Customer than it does to engage a Fan. But companies always forget the Fans, and they rarely direct marketing strategy and marketing actions towards them. Businesses should be channelling around 70 per cent of their marketing efforts and budget towards this group.

A few years ago, we worked with a client in the beauty industry. They had over five years of turning Strangers into Customers under their belt, and they had hit a bit of a rut.

'We need more customers', they told us. 'New marketing ideas, new marketing channels.'

What they didn't think to focus on were the 12 000 customers they had already collected over the past five years. Marketing to this group cost a fraction of the amount it would take to market to Strangers, and increased their sales by 2.5 times month on month because they didn't have to convince a Stranger to try their products.

They'd already tried the products! They were already Fans. They just needed a bit of engagement and encouragement to buy again.

The journey

So now we know the different phases a customer goes through on their journey from a Stranger to a Fan. The next most important part of the model is understanding where marketing fits into the context. The purpose of marketing is to help a Customer continue from one stage to the next. The strength of your marketing determines how many people evolve from a Stranger to a Visitor, and then a Visitor to a Lead, and so forth.

No one marketing method is going to work from the start to the end of the journey. Remember that. As soon as you start trying to fit this entire journey into one activity, you will fail.

Your website is busy turning Visitors into Leads. You just want them to pick up the phone or send that enquiry. After that, you can personally take them through to becoming a Customer. A website that's trying to do everything, including selling, could be your leaky bucket, leaking Visitors out of your website and onto someone else's.

How strong is your marketing?

If 100 people are introduced to your business through a Google Ad, and they all click on it, and they all send you an enquiry, all become Customers and then become raving Fans, I want you to give me a call ASAP. Because I'm certain that, for most businesses, 100 impressions on a Google Ad leads to around 0.007 Fans. Not 100.

How do I know this?

Well, as someone moves from one touchpoint to another, they are either going to continue their journey or they are going to leave. The rate at which they continue their journey is called the conversion rate — and that rate is, in essence, how good your marketing is.

A conversion rate is the most important number in this entire model. It is going to be your benchmark for how good or bad your marketing is at any point on the customer journey. It is easy to measure, and it is easy to compare with others, so when I say 100 people start as Strangers and only 0.007 people make it to the end, I know this because the average:

- click-through rate (Strangers to Visitors) on a Google Ad is 2.5 per cent

- conversion rate on a website (Visitors to Leads) is 3.5 per cent

- conversion rate for a service-based business (Leads to Customers) is 40 per cent

- time someone gives a 9 or 10 out of 10 on a customer service survey (Customers to Fans) is 20 per cent.

And these are the averages. Chances are your business is quite a way from delivering these numbers.

Similarly, working backwards from these numbers will show us just how many clicks the Google Ads will need to generate that one Fan for you.

$$((1/0.2)/0.4)/0.035$$

The answer is 357 clicks, which will probably cost you around US$3.33 each, which is $1188.81.

Conversion rates are where this entire model is going to focus. How can you change your future by improving the marketing you are doing at each touchpoint to improve your conversation rates? Because it will genuinely have an incredible difference.

If your business is delivering the above conversion rates across your customer journey, but you put all your focus and time into improving the conversion rate of your website, so much so that it now converts at 7 per cent instead of 3.5 per cent, this lowers your acquisition cost to $594. Or, to go the other way, it doubles the number of Fans you'll get if you start with 100 Google Ad impressions.

So, the power of what we are about to go through in this book is astronomical. Just examining your customer journey as this linear system is going to change the way you see marketing forever.

The <u>Very</u> Simple Principle

Wondering what the last ingredient of this model is? This Very Simple Principle is going to make so much sense you'll want a refund from the purchase of this book. We've explained the commitments that need to accompany this model, we've introduced the customer journey and the power of conversion rates, and now the number one thing you need to do is beat your marketing bottleneck.

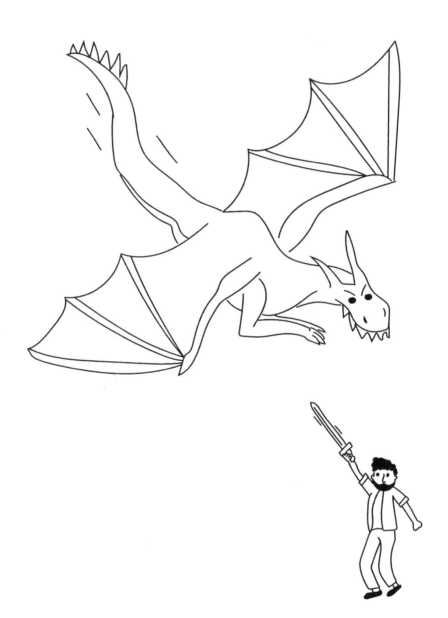

THREE

BEAT YOUR MARKETING BOTTLENECK

Julia and Simon officially hold the record for the best performing sales team after implementing this model into their business. And it was not even as fully developed as it is now. They used the more elementary, minimum viable product (MVP) version I was testing and developing in late 2019.

I was attending a private community event in Perth when I first met Julia and Simon. As we got to talking they began telling me a bit about their struggles with their business over the last few years since they moved to a bigger premises in Willagee.

When Julia and Simon started their business six years ago, they were riding on the coattails of Simon's personal network in the industry. As distributors and manufacturers of high-load bearings, seals and so forth, their market size was finite and Simon, who had been in the industry for nearly a decade, knew almost every single potential Customer.

This kind of business kick-off isn't uncommon. Starting a new brand in an industry you're already familiar with is how hundreds of entrepreneurs and founders dive into ownership — and many have fallen into the same hardships that Julia and Simon had when it came to scaling.

Five years into the business, Julia and Simon were ready to take it to the next level. They had grown out of their small workshop and wanted to move to a bigger space, make more products and grow their team. It's the entrepreneurial dream, right?

So, they made the move and hired more staff (estimators, receptionists, tradespeople). Simon was finally able to work on product development, and Julia had taken off all her entrepreneur hats, but one: the marketing one. To meet their revenue targets, Julia knew they had to get some new customers in the door. And quickly.

Then Julia made a marketing move that almost every small-to-medium enterprise (SME) I've ever worked with has done. She called a digital marketing agency. 'I was given absolute guarantees that an aggressive SEO strategy was going to quadruple our leads', Julia explained to me at the event. 'They told me it could take up to a year to see results, and it would cost us $2500 per month.'

'And ... how's it been going?' I asked.

'Yeah, good!' Julia bluffed. 'Our keywords are seriously up.' Then there was silence. Let's just say the look on their faces told me that, although keyword rankings were up, sales were not.

The marketing promise

You've probably had the same issues when it comes to growing your business. If you're like Simon, you've built your business through genuine relationships and good word of mouth. That's awesome. And it's going to be a big foundation for your business growth for years to come. But to get the growth you want next, you're going to need more clients. More clients and more sales and more Fans — which means very good marketing, which is why you picked up this book.

Good marketing is the key to increasing your revenue. It is the key to Customers understanding your products and services, and it's the key to how they will enhance their business or their life. With good marketing, they'll be able to find you when they need you, they'll be able to communicate with you and they'll be able to tell other people about you.

With good marketing, you'll be able to reach your goals. So, what happens when good marketing isn't helping you reach your goals? What happens when the money you are spending on marketing doesn't lead to more clients and more sales and more Fans? Where do you go next?

Julia invested a lot of money into, arguably, good marketing, and paid top experts to help her grow her revenue. Yet, she was nowhere near closer to her goals than when she started. She knew her business needed new Customers, ones outside of Simon's network and new to their products and services. She was convinced by her marketing agency that she needed to 'dominate' and 'saturate' her market by ranking first for all the keywords in her industry, and by doing this, she would increase her revenue. But she didn't.

When I started working with small businesses, I thought marketing to Strangers was how you increased revenue. But I was wrong.

Over time, I realised that, whilst attracting Strangers to your business was incredibly important, there were so many other customer interactions where you needed to employ marketing techniques to generate revenue.

And those were just as important (if not more important) than marketing to Strangers. But small businesses don't realise that because marketing agencies continue shouting from the rooftops that their marketing specialty guarantees an increase in revenue. Tell me, when did investing in marketing become so correlated with revenue?

It is so ingrained in marketing rhetoric and within the marketing industry that I am not surprised so many foreclosed businesses cite poor marketing as their #2 reason for failure.

The marketing promise is a trap. Often, I help a small business double or triple their revenue without any investment in marketing at all. (What?! That's impossible!)

How? By helping them beat the bottlenecks stopping Customers from making the journey from a Stranger to becoming their biggest Fan. And trust me, only once you've beaten those bottlenecks can every dollar you spend on marketing make a difference to your bottom line.

Such as it did for a leader of a kingdom far, far away. Where a troublesome bottleneck was causing his own quest for success to fall terribly short.

A slightly different journey

On a very cold morning, inside a very cold castle in a land far, far away, a short, dark-haired man wearing a green velvet outfit stood on a plinth in front of 100 men.

'My future bride', he announced, looking around the room at armoured-clad soldiers, 'is being held captive! By a monstrous dragon! She is in a faraway castle, in the highest room of the tallest tower. And the person to rescue her and bring her home to me will be generously rewarded!'

He raised his sword into the air and yelled, 'Huzzah!' This was met with a roar of agreeable 'huzzahs!' and shouts and the raising of 100 swords and the official start of the lord's quest.

The clattering knights shuffled out of the castle and began mounting horses and ponies whilst the lord retired to his chambers to relax and wait for the arrival of his future bride.

He waited there for hours. Which turned into days. And then turned into weeks.

'*Where* is she?!' he shouted as he burst into his clerk's quarters. 'Where are my knights with my bride! Why aren't they back?' he demanded. When the clerk started to speak, the lord interjected, 'I don't care, send more! Send more knights! Better knights! I don't care what it costs!' And he stormed out of the room.

More knights were deployed on the quest the next day and still there was no word about his bride. Again, hours turned into days and days turned into weeks. And nothing was happening. It was frustrating. It was *infuriating*. (Now you know how Julia must be feeling.)

'*Why has nobody returned with my future bride?*' the lord demanded once again to the timid clerk.

'I'm … I'm not sure … my Lord', he stammered in a squeaky voice. 'It could be the dragon … maybe. Or they may have perished of thirst … ' he finished.

'*Thirst!*' The lord bellowed, 'What do you mean *thirst?!*'

'The … desert. They have to cross the desert', the clerk continued, 'and pass through blistering winds.'

This confused the lord. He was pretty sure the way to acquire his bride was to send knights on a journey to rescue her. Now he was being told that there's more? The knights have to be supplied with water and supplies and goodness knows what else?

The lord considered (briefly) giving up the entire quest, but then he remembered why he started the quest in the first place. To rescue the princess from the dragon.

'*Give me a map!*' the lord yelled. 'I want to know where the knights are perishing, so we can send better, more capable knights out. Ones that can return me my bride.' That's what happens when you leave an important job to fools, he thought.

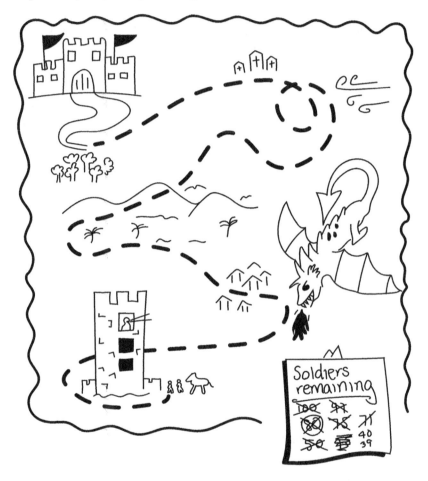

When the clerk finally returned with a map, the lord peered at it eagerly. 'You sent out 285 knights', the clerk wrote on the map next to the castle. 'Five men drowned in the moat under the weight of their armour leaving the castle.'

'Fools', the lord mumbled pitilessly.

'Twenty-four of them', the clerk continued, 'lost their horses between the blistering winds and the scorching deserts. A further 30 of them died from dehydration crossing the scorching desert. And 210 didn't make it past the dragon to the tower staircase. And finally', he finished, 'the 16 that did avoid the dragon seem to have perished somewhere between the highest room and the tallest tower, either from sustained injury or a lack of sustenance. Nobody seems to have gotten to the princess yet.'

There was a moment of awkward silence.

'How exactly did the 16 men get past that blasted dragon?'

'Ah ... Good customer service it appears', said the clerk. 'They talked their way past the dragon.'

'Interesting ... ' the lord murmured. 'If we can get more knights to pass the dragon, we will absolutely get to the princess.' He got up suddenly to leave the room. 'Teach them! I will assemble another army. They can leave on the morrow.'

The lord felt very confident indeed.

With a clear overview of the complete journey from castle to princess, identifying what was stopping the knights from succeeding wasn't hard at all. And the same can be said for your business. Once you gain a clear picture of your entire customer journey from Stranger to Fan, any touchpoints deterring your customers can be quickly identified and overcome so that the biggest number of people can make their way from start to finish and have the biggest impact on your business success.

Julia's bottleneck

'Do you mind if I send you a quiz?' I asked Julia and Simon at the end of the evening. 'It's just a marketing quiz. It might help you make sense of what you can do next to build business.'

Logically, what Julia was executing for her business made complete sense in the simplified formula for business growth. More Strangers introduced to your business = more Customers. The problem was that she didn't know to examine her entire customer journey to see what was happening to those Strangers, or even if they were the right ones for her business.

What she was about to discover was that investing in attracting Strangers was probably the last thing she needed to do — as was sending more and more ill-equipped knights on the princess quest, in the case of the lord bachelor.

When I sent through the quiz (the essence of which is at the end of this chapter), I wasn't sure how quickly Julia would get around to completing it. She had two young daughters and a business to run, and diving into your marketing inadequacies was not normally a fun, Friday evening activity. But, much to my surprise, Julia's completed quiz was sitting in my inbox the next morning. Her only words to accompany the attachment were, 'Please help!'

As a business owner, you don't usually have the time to tune into the small stuff in your business: how people answer the phone, how long it takes to produce a quote, how your products are referred to on social media, how photographs are taken, etc. Chances are you review marketing every month, maybe every few months or perhaps just when things are a bit tight.

So, when Julia took the Bottleneck Quiz, and it became glaringly obvious that her sure-thing, 100 per cent conversion-rate sales division was no longer delivering those results for the business, she was seriously panicked.

When business was flying, Simon was winning almost every job he quoted on. He was taking clients to dinner, he was going on sites to meet people and have a chat. When the business was steadily profitable and growing, Simon moved into product development (his passion).

Except his successors were not performing nearly as well as Simon. All talented engineers, the team would receive an enquiry, estimate on the job and send a quote to the customer.

Done and completed. That was their job: to produce an estimate for a lead and send it back to them. Except their conversion rate was well down: it was close to 10 per cent. Or that's what Julia could see from a collection of mismatched Excel spreadsheets and email threads. Her business had gone from a near 100 per cent conversion rate on every enquiry to a 10 per cent conversion rate in just ten months. Regardless of how many new Customers were coming in, it was a disaster. Their competitors were probably having a field day.

Beating your marketing bottleneck

The ending of Julia and Simon's story is a good one. After identifying that their biggest bottleneck was converting Leads to Customers, they put Simon back in the sales chair and developed a marketing and sales process that was codified to ensure anyone could complete it with the same success Simon was having ten months ago. And they set up parameters to keep a constant eye on it.

After beating this bottleneck and improving revenue significantly, Julia took the Bottleneck Quiz again to pinpoint her next challenge to work through. She repeated the process until her investment in SEO was finally leading to a return she was proud to boast to a stranger about at a networking event.

And the crazy part is they didn't have to spend big or risk big to make it happen.

Clarity on the problem, consistency in the process, commitment to the outcome, communication amongst the team and constant improvement enabled them to methodically work through each lead and create a winning process for their conversion using marketing. The great news is that you can do it too. And it all starts with identifying and beating your bottleneck.

By doing this you are going to double, triple, quadruple the success of your efforts at that touchpoint of your customer journey *and* give every single Stranger the best probability of becoming your biggest Fan.

Dedicating your entire marketing budget to fixing your bottlenecks is a controversial move, but one that you won't regret. Here's why.

Small changes have amplified results

With Julia's conversion rate from Leads to Customers sitting at 10 per cent, what could doubling that conversion rate mean? Going from 10 per cent to 20 per cent doesn't seem like a whole lot when it used to be close to 100 per cent, but by doubling the number of successful lead conversions, they are doubling their revenue each month. And creating a flow-on effect in the customer journey from Customer through to Fan.

If our lord and his clerk were able to increase the success rate at the dragon interaction by even 1 per cent, that would be an additional three knights on the journey up the stairs to the princess and a 16 per cent increase in the likelihood one was going to reach the princess! Now those are odds you'll want to invest your marketing budget in.

Focus saves you money

Time and time again we are reminded that focusing on one thing at a time will always lead to a much better outcome than spreading your energy across multiple things. Gary Keller and Jay Papasan even wrote *The One Thing*, a whole book, about this simple idea: 'It is those who concentrate on but one thing at a time who advance in this world.'

The day you stop doing everything that falls under 'marketing' and just focus on one thing is the day you are going to feel like you're actually getting somewhere.

As we talk about back in chapter 1, focus is a really big problem that small-business owners face. Not just in marketing, but in everything. There's so much to do and not enough time. And when it comes to marketing, businesses spread themselves thin because they believe the opportunity cost of not doing social media or not competing on SEO or not writing a blog is way too great.

But that's not you! Focusing on one bottleneck at a time is going to mean you are deliberately investing in something that is going to increase your conversion rates.

Marketing to Strangers seldom ends in revenue

If I haven't convinced you already, spending money attracting Strangers at the start of your customer journey rarely leads to an increase in revenue. Not unless the rest of your marketing system is leak-free. Most businesses will usually turn to attracting Strangers in times of slow growth, believing they've reached the natural limits of their existing resources, and that the only way up is to find more Strangers.

This idea is stopping so many businesses from breaking through the ceiling of growth to reach their full potential. If all you are doing to solve your growth problem is attempting to attract new Customers, you are basically filling a leaky bucket with more and more water and wondering why it isn't holding the liquid you are pouring into it.

By focusing all your budget on blocking those holes and fixing those bottlenecks, you will set your business up for the best return on investment when it comes time to find new Strangers for your business. You're equipping every single one of them with the right tools they need to make that treacherous journey.

No more stabbing in the dark

Most entrepreneurs have a clear vision. Their problem is that they make the mistake of relying on new Customers to achieve that vision. In most cases, leaders end up frustrated, with no obvious answers as to why they can't achieve the growth they want. Is it product? Is it price? Is it competitors? Marketing? Imagery? Packaging? Sales?

By identifying which aspects of your customer journey are letting you down, you will gain clarity regarding where your bottlenecks are and the focus areas where you need to start making improvements. When you clarify your customer journey, you will be able to make better decisions and help everyone in your organisation clearly see what the goal is and how you will get there: no more stabbing in the dark.

There will always be an area of your marketing that could be performing better. At first, you will invest your marketing budget there, and improve every touchpoint until it hits or exceeds industry standards. From there, you can invest in attracting Strangers more confidently and reach your goals faster and in a more controlled manner.

INTRODUCING THE BOTTLENECK QUIZ

Imagine if you had a mechanism for quickly and easily identifying the fire-breathing dragon gobbling up your customers on their journey from Stranger to Fan?

Well, after many years, surveys, data and (peril-less) quests, we developed a qualitative quiz that would predict the quantitative realities of a small-business marketing bottleneck.

The results of this quiz will give you a pathway for your marketing attention by ranking the different touchpoints in order of what's not going well to what is going well, so you can begin fighting your biggest bottleneck immediately. Once you've tackled one, you can take the quiz again and move onto the next one until your revenue begins to soar.

To take the full Bottleneck Quiz, visit verygoodmarketing.com.au.

The rapid Bottleneck Quiz

Circle the answer you believe to be most truthful on the quiz below. Use the scoring key at the end of the quiz to find your result.

Everyone in our organisation can explain what our business does in one sentence.

| Strongly Disagree | Disagree | Unsure | Agree | Strongly Agree |

We know the best marketing method for our business.

| Strongly Disagree | Disagree | Unsure | Agree | Strongly Agree |

We know the return on investment we get from our marketing spend.

| Strongly Disagree | Disagree | Unsure | Agree | Strongly Agree |

Turning Strangers into Visitors   Score:

Our website generates business for us.

| Strongly Disagree | Disagree | Unsure | Agree | Strongly Agree |

We know the conversion rate of our website.

| Strongly Disagree | Disagree | Unsure | Agree | Strongly Agree |

Visitors to our website know what we do in five seconds or less.

| Strongly Disagree | Disagree | Unsure | Agree | Strongly Agree |

Turning Visitors into Leads   Score:

Our sales team works toward clear goals and targets.

| Strongly Disagree | Disagree | Unsure | Agree | Strongly Agree |

We know our sales win/loss ratio.

| Strongly Disagree | Disagree | Unsure | Agree | Strongly Agree |

We have a clear sales process that is delivered consistently.

| Strongly Disagree | Disagree | Unsure | Agree | Strongly Agree |

Turning Leads into Customers   Score:

We deliver our products and services consistently.				
Strongly Disagree	Disagree	Unsure	Agree	Strongly Agree

We receive a lot of good reviews.				
Strongly Disagree	Disagree	Unsure	Agree	Strongly Agree

We have many loyal Customers who spread the word about our business.				
Strongly Disagree	Disagree	Unsure	Agree	Strongly Agree

Turning Customers into Fans   Score:

We know who our biggest advocates for our business are.				
Strongly Disagree	Disagree	Unsure	Agree	Strongly Agree

We communicate regularly to our biggest advocates.				
Strongly Disagree	Disagree	Unsure	Agree	Strongly Agree

There is a system in place that generates reviews for our business.				
Strongly Disagree	Disagree	Unsure	Agree	Strongly Agree

Turning Fans into Jam   Score:

Scoring

Add up your answers using the following key and fill in the score box on each of the above question groups. The lowest score represents your biggest bottleneck.

Strongly Disagree	Disagree	Unsure	Agree	Strongly Agree
0	1	2	3	4

My biggest Bottleneck is…

The ticket to arriving at your goals

Whilst Julia struggled to turn Leads into Customers, other organisations thrive in this area, but may need help to engage their existing Customers. You may be bottled up somewhere completely different. Whatever result you received, remember that identifying the problem is the first step to being able to overcome it. The next step is fixing it, and this is where the real fun begins.

FAQ: Everything you might be wondering about The Very Good Marketing Framework

What if I got the same score in my Bottleneck Quiz for two areas?

If you finished the Bottleneck Quiz with two equal priorities, my recommendation would be to choose the one earliest in the customer journey to work on next. That will enable you to open traffic to the next stage of the journey.

What if the marketing industry changes? Does this framework become obsolete?

Marketing changes all the time. Or at least the techniques do. But the stages of a customer journey are unlikely to change, and the system itself will remain consistent, as will the techniques and approaches in this book.

So you want me to direct my entire marketing budget to my bottleneck?

Yes!

What do I do with the marketing I currently have underway?

I get it. It's a big risk just ditching all your marketing methods right now to focus in on something new. If you're not comfortable shutting marketing off, you can continue it, but only if:

♦ you believe you are doing a good job, and you are putting in at least 70 per cent of possible effort into it

♦ it is working to bring you business

♦ stopping it is going to cause more problems

♦ you're confident it is going to be a big part of your marketing strategy going forward.

As you work towards beating your current bottleneck, you may find you'll need to redirect some of your resources (time, staff, money) towards that goal, so keep that in mind.

I have absolutely no budget for marketing. Is it worth reading the rest of the book?

Good question. Building strong foundations in marketing and sales is probably one of the most important things you are going to do for your business. Fortunately, there are a lot of things in this book that will not cost any money; they just might take up some of your time. So if you're ready to invest some of your sweat equity and give this a really good go, then please, read on.

The cost of not doing so could be much more.

What should my marketing budget be as a small-business owner?

One of the questions I get a lot from small-business owners is just how much of your revenue you should allocate to marketing. How do I know what marketing investment is required to reach my goals?

According to the Small Business Development Corporation, SME owners and founders report spending 2 per cent to 4 per cent of revenue on average each year on marketing. They also report that it is the first thing to go in times of financial stress and the easiest thing to waste.

If your business is currently profitable and meeting your cash flow requirements, I would recommend putting aside at least 3 per cent each month to invest in marketing. I don't care if that is $100 per month or $15 000 per month, this amount needs to be dedicated to beating your bottlenecks first, before any other marketing to Strangers is attempted.

So am I going to have to do all of this myself?

When we start working through a plan to execute a marketing strategy, I'm not going to expect you to open a Google Ads account over breakfast and start choosing broad match and long-tail keywords (whatever those mean, amiright?). But you do need to know whether Google Ads is a good strategy for your business. Then it is up to you to take action and hire that Google Ads company.

The biggest mistake you can make as a Visionary is not having a strategy, and not taking actions towards implementing it.

Does this framework contradict everything I have read before on marketing?

Because consumer patterns and channels for communication evolve all the time, marketing has become increasingly complex. And the best minds in marketing are working hard at simplifying it. Finding patterns. Sharing those patterns with you.

I love a good marketing book, but what I love more is a plan to execute it.

And with a small marketing budget, a small amount of time and a whole lot of risk, a good marketing theory is just not enough for a small business.

Many well-intentioned marketing theorists have the best ideas in the world that are never implemented because the gap between theory and strategy and action are just too far apart.

This practical information in this book is going to take you from strategy and theory towards action. A very good friend of mine told me that good marketing foundations are like a rock-climbing camming device. If it is strong enough and implemented correctly, you can climb past it, but will always be caught by it in the case of a fall. You won't fall below it.

Imagine climbing a mountain of the latest marketing trends and theories without a camming device. As soon as you get distracted, lose focus, momentum, energy, resources, you'll fall all the way back down to the bottom.

PART II
BEATING YOUR BOTTLENECKS

Congratulations on making it to Part II. So far, all we've really done is identify that there is a problem, and that your business has a bottleneck that needs to be fixed ASAP.

Which makes Part II all the more exciting, because now I'm going to give you the exact recipe for fixing it. Remember that you'll need to jump to the chapter that matches the biggest bottleneck you have right now. Once you've fixed it and you can see it working for your business, you can move on to the next one.

Like a choose-your-own-adventure novel, Part II is about tackling each of your bottlenecks one at a time. So, turn to the chapter that best represents your current bottleneck rather than working your way through the book sequentially. This is going to get you the quickest results for your time and budget.

The key is to take it slow! Big change takes time. But, oh, is it worth it!

FOUR

HOW TO TURN A STRANGER INTO A VISITOR

Let me tell you about the conversation I have most frequently with my small-business clients. It's usually towards the end of a website-build project, after we've been floating the idea that they need to think about *how* someone is going to find their website. 'We can talk about it later', they normally say.

So we come to the end of the website build, everyone is really excited about it. It's gone live (it looks great), it's been sent to mum and dad and the rest of the organisation, and posted on LinkedIn. At which point I'll suggest that we 'have a chat about how people are going to discover your website'.

And I get a few puzzled looks.

'It's live now, so people just go to our domain name, and they will find our website', I receive in return.

'Yeah, but how do they know your domain name? You're trying to grow your customer base, and attract new customers who don't know you exist. You might need to start looking at SEO or digital ads now.'

The reality of this always hits pretty hard. Thousands of dollars on a website and it doesn't even come with customers?

When it comes to marketing, attracting Strangers is the beginning of a process that can't continue without that first step. So how exactly do you attract people to your website? And, in a broader sense, how do you attract Strangers to your business?

What I've found, time and time again, is most business owners who want Strangers as a mechanism for growth often have a bottleneck elsewhere. Without the rest of your marketing system operating effectively, it could be catastrophic to go out and attract Strangers. This is because they are expensive, and often there is a finite number of them in your target market.

This happened to Ashley.

Marketing gone cold

Ashley and I met because he was fatigued by his business. He'd spent a decade creating a highly sophisticated cooling system for potable water. Essentially it was a heat pump cooling unit but for water instead of air, where any water lines going to taps or showers could be cooled down continuously. 'Why is this even required?' you might be thinking. 'Cold water always comes out of the taps. Surely hot water is the harder bit?'

Well, I thought the same thing, but Ashley explained to me that in hotter climates (such as anywhere in the northern parts of Australia), potable water can get up to 50 degrees, making taps and showers virtually unusable. For campsites, towns and mining facilities in warm climates, it can be impossible to cool this water down, and many residents painstakingly fill buckets with water hours ahead of when they need them just to avoid the hot temperatures.

And that isn't even the really bad part. Many facilities located in warm climates rely on essential safety elements like safety showers to prevent injuries from spills, etc. What happens when the water to those safety showers is too hot to use?

Pretty essential, huh?

Ashley has been developing these units for years. In fact, he has entire systems that can be installed on site to remove the risk of bacteria growth inside warm pipes, circulate fresh water and operate off the grid. But after years and years of trying to sell these units to mining companies and other organisations across the country, he has had very little success, and when we met, he was close to shutting up shop.

I was blown away by the products he had created, and saw very quickly the need for them, not just for the wellbeing of residents in those areas without access to cool water, but for essential safety services.

Ashley, however, was a Technician. He was an expert in his technical craft and, therefore, his attempts to market his products had not done them justice. His website read like a technical manual, his products weren't easy to understand and, to put it simply, he wasn't good at explaining what he did. This meant that every effort over the last decade to attract Strangers to his business through social media, networking events and direct business development fell on deaf ears.

Ashley's marketing method looked a bit like this:

1. He would find a relevant person within an organisation through his networks or through LinkedIn.

2. He would reach out for a meeting.

3. If they said yes, he would meet them for a coffee and bring along a brochure and direct them to his website.

4. He wouldn't hear from them again.

One of two things was most likely happening here. First, Ashley's conversation, brochure and website were too complex or overwhelming for his meeting recipient. They didn't understand the product and didn't know what to do next.

Alternatively, the person thought his products were fantastic and needed them right away. So they sent the brochure and website to their purchasing manager who didn't understand it at all — especially without Ashley's guidance.

This was happening time and time again. And after a decade of meeting people, introducing himself and having these meetings, Ashley was running out of Strangers to target.

So if you've made it here, ready to beat the Strangers to Visitors bottleneck, then congratulations! This is usually the last piece of a marketing puzzle, and one of the most rewarding to implement.

Together, we are going to gain clarity on what marketing methods are going to be most effective for your business and how to implement them in a way that creates focus and impact and stops unnecessary money wastage.

The art of attraction

The journey to take someone from being a Stranger to a Visitor of your website, your social media page or your bricks-and-mortar store can take many forms. In fact, the marketing channels and methods available are bigger than you may even realise, and are changing every day.

The task at hand is taking a complete Stranger to a place where they can learn more.

Sound simple?

The ability to achieve this relies on two things:

◆ getting in front of the right people (at the right time, in the right place)

◆ convincing them to take action (the message).

Your ability to attract Strangers to your business will depend on you getting both these things right and putting as much effort as you can into it.

Take Google Ads as an example. Using this marketing channel to successfully turn Strangers into Visitors to your website relies on you:

◆ targeting the right keywords, having the right bid strategy, having a good budget (i.e. getting in front of the right people)

◆ convincing them to click on your ad over someone else's (take action).

And once you have perfected it for one channel, you can perfect it for another, and another, until you have a diverse spread of marketing 'nets' out there ready to attract the Customers and Fans your business needs to thrive.

So the next three questions I am going to answer for you are:

How do I get in front of the right Strangers?

How do I convince them to take action?

What are my next steps?

These three elements are key to building an effective marketing strategy that attracts strangers to your business.

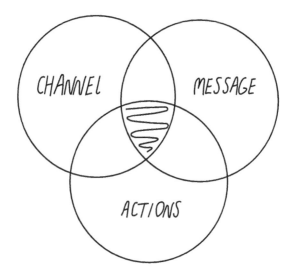

Channel: How do I get in front of the right people?

Let's start by dispelling the myth that you have to be a marketing expert to answer this question. You have all the knowledge you need to make your marketing work, and with the right steps in place, any other answers you need aren't far off. I've found, time and time again, that business owners equipped with good marketing foundations have more success than marketing 'experts' coming in fresh to a business. The only thing missing from your reality is a marketing framework so you can base decisions on a clear set of actions. You know your business better than anyone, and when you combine that knowledge with a grip on good marketing, anything is possible.

In his book *Get Back in the Box: Innovation from the inside out*, Douglas Rushkoff makes the point that companies need to stop looking everywhere else for answers. He urges readers to 'stop solving your problems from the outside in'. His point is that companies have a significant amount of experience and knowledge within their organisation that no external consultant or advertiser can match. That knowledge is what leads to success.

If you are a normal small business, you've probably got to where you are with a less-than-perfect approach to finding new customers. When you were getting your business off the ground, you were fastidious regarding the delivery of your products and went above and beyond for the customers you had. As a result, word of mouth became the sole source of your growth. Maybe it still is, but if you're reading this book, you've probably reached the limits of what that can provide, or else you have tried to supplement it through other means with little success.

A problem for most business owners is that they take a scattergun approach to attracting Strangers, rather than selecting a method with deliberation or giving a chosen method sufficient attention and commitment. When business owners do this, there is always the potential for them to feel regret and exasperation: 'Well, I tried something that someone told me to try, and it didn't work — what's the point of taking another risk. Maybe our product isn't quite right.'

It doesn't take much for an organisation to get off track in the hustle and bustle of everyday activities. Businesses can easily become distracted with opportunities, competitors, a new idea, a new product and poor advice (which looked like good advice at the time).

Your job is to find the right marketing channels for your business with focus: slowly and methodically running experiments to know for certain whether a marketing channel/message/execution mix is the right one for you. Eliminating distractions is the only way to do this.

What is a marketing channel?

Marketing channels are the mechanisms, the paths or the ways a complete Stranger becomes a Visitor to your business. Many of them are online, some are offline, and some are ambiguous and immeasurable. The scope and breadth of them is vast, so it is important to be granular when identifying what your business is currently doing to find Strangers so that you can critically examine it and give or retract your attention.

A really easy way to examine marketing channels available for turning Strangers into Visitors is by breaking it down by intention. Which channels are designed to 'interrupt' Strangers (push) with your business and which ones are designed to 'match up' Strangers (pull) with your brand after an intended purchase.

Push channels

Push channels interrupt Strangers going about their daily life. They stumble across your business, and you show them a solution to a problem they didn't realise they had.

Pull channels

Pull channels meet a Stranger when they are searching for a solution. These customers are considered 'warm' (i.e. they are ready to buy something to solve their problem). They are often choosing between multiple providers or searching for a solution they aren't sure exists.

Push	Pull
Display advertising	SEO
Social media advertising	SEM
Video pre-roll advertising	Directory listings
Television advertising	Word of mouth
Print advertising	Guests blogging
Billboard advertising	Organic social media
Product placement	
Big stunts/guerrilla marketing	
Letterbox drops	
Sponsorship	
Influencers/affiliates	
Networking events	
Proactive business development	
Trade shows	

Perhaps you have tried some of these for your business before? Breaking them down by intention may enlighten you as to why your campaigns may have worked or not worked effectively, and give you clarity into where your marketing message may have been ineffective.

Successful businesses (businesses that have made it past the chasm into bigger business) have an effective mix of attraction strategies across both columns, ensuring they can target Strangers based on their demographics and behaviours across multiple channels.

Very advanced businesses will use these marketing methods to not only turn Strangers into Visitors but also turn 'abandoned' Visitors into Leads, capturing people who have come to their website and left without progressing. If you have ever visited a website one day and seen an advertisement for the same company on social media the next, this is an example of the display advertising channel re-targeting you based on your visitor behaviour. The opportunities for your business are incredible.

But they are also almost infinite, which is why it is important for us to get focused.

Eliminating the scattergun approach

Most companies already have everything they need to achieve the growth they desire. Their products are exceptional, they have loyal Customers and they are consistently innovating. These businesses are sitting on diamond mines, but the quickest way to lose your diamond mine is to get bored, distracted or over-ambitious or focus on what everyone else is doing. Marketing your business can tell the same story. You already have amazing products and services (you've come this far), but the number of marketing channels, messages and technology available to you is overwhelming. You just need focus, and I am going to show you exactly how to achieve that.

Bullseye

During my time working with small businesses, I have uncovered three broad themes related to marketing channels.

First, most entrepreneurs will only consider using marketing channels with which they are already familiar. This manifests itself in refusing to use the latest social media channels if you haven't experienced them personally, or else using inappropriate methods just because you use it every day, without regard to your target market. These businesses end up focusing on the same channels and ignore other promising ways of attracting Strangers and generating growth.

Second, it is hard to predict the marketing channels that will work best. You can make educated guesses, but until you start running experiments and making commitments, it is difficult to tell which channel is the best one for you right now. The exercise I am going to introduce next will encourage you to brainstorm all channels, investigate a handful and then laser focus on a single channel that appears to be the most promising. When considering channels, try not to dismiss them as irrelevant for your company. Each traction channel has worked for all kinds of businesses all over the world. The right channel can sometimes be the most under-utilised one.

Lastly, everyone gives up way too early. A perfect example of this is social media — it is one of the channels that pays great dividends, but can take years to gain traction in. So many people give up when they do not see instant results, and they switch to something else. Full commitment to your marketing channel to the exclusion of everything else is required to gain the traction you need to succeed.

Bullseye is the exercise we designed to help you create focus around turning Strangers into Visitors, to ensure you choose the channels that enable you get in front of the right Customers, every time.

Exercise: Bullseye

Time required: 2–3 hours

Stakeholders: Leadership team, marketing professionals, team members

Equipment: Whiteboard, markers

Set-up: Draw the following image on your whiteboard so that it takes up most of the space.

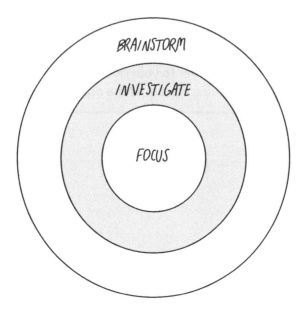

Method

1. Brainstorm: All good ideas start with opening our minds to what is possible. Use the outer ring of the bullseye diagram to brainstorm all the marketing channels that are available to your business. These could include some listed in the table on page 79 or brand new ones that you have discovered. This part of the exercise should only take you five minutes.

2. Investigate: The next step in this exercise is to critically look at the channels you have brainstormed to identify which ones are more suited to your business. Using your target market as a guide, which channels are more likely to attract Customers to your business? Which ones are lower hanging fruit? Which ones may be more complex? You should aim for between four and six ideas in your middle ring. These are the channels you are going to investigate. Choosing these channels should take around ten minutes.

3. Focus: Lastly, you are going to use the results of your investigation to focus on just one of these marketing channels for 90 days to the exclusion of all others. This enables you to create focus, amplify your efforts and work out once and for all whether this marketing channel is the answer to your question: 'How do I get my product/service in front of the right people?'

So how do you choose just one marketing channel?

It's easy to say, 'just pick one marketing channel', but how do you actually do this? You need to have a clear idea *why* this channel is at the top of your list and how it fits in with your overall marketing strategy. Have you tried it before with some success? Have you heard about it from other people? Here are some things you should think about.

Target market volumes

This is where you think about how well you know your target market. How many of them use this channel? Getting precise numbers is tricky, so consider how else you can answer the question: 'Does my target market use [this channel] and, if so, how many of them use it?' Many marketing channels already make this information available; for example, social media platforms have demographic breakdowns of users, advertising companies utilising mediums like billboards or magazines can provide marketing breakdowns, and Google can shed the light on a lot of the gaps in between. For example, if Ashley was considering using TikTok as a strategy, matching his target market (purchasing officers for big mining companies) to TikTok user demographics may not give very favourable numbers.

Competitors

Are your competitors using this channel? Are they having success? If they aren't using it, is there a reason why? If they are bigger than your company, is there a chance they have tried it to no avail or is there a secret opportunity here? If you are investigating a channel that is extremely popular (for example, you are a home builder and you are looking into spending money on Google advertising using keywords like 'new home builder'), your effectiveness will be diminished because of the numerous other companies like yours all vying for the same click.

Feasibility

How much will it cost and what resources are required to give 105 per cent focus and effort to this marketing channel to get results? Some advertising mediums, such as television advertising or guerrilla marketing, may be very expensive to execute and, combined with the target market numbers, just may not stack up. Others, such as Facebook or LinkedIn advertising, may have a better cost argument because investment can start small and grow upon success with little risk.

Implementation

How will you roll this marketing method out? What resources will you need? What is the timing? Thinking about how you will implement this method will give you a quick overview of what parts need to be in place before you can start gaining traction. An SEO strategy, for example, may require an external marketing expert to be hired, plus 12 months of investment before results are harvested. Therefore, if you need results now, it may not be the best implementation strategy for your business. This leads me to the final thing you need to investigate ...

Goals

Will this channel help you reach your goals? If you have a goal to deliver ten leads this month to your sales team, which channels are going to get you those leads in time? How can you work backwards from the end of your customer journey system to identify how many Strangers you need to acquire to turn the biggest number possible into Fans?

Investigation example: Ashley

Ashley was considering attending the upcoming WA Mining Expo with his water-cooling system. To determine whether this marketing channel was going to be an effective one for his business, he undertook an investigation into it and researched the following areas.

Investigation into the WA Mining Expo	Findings
Overview	The WA Mining Expo is WA's largest dedicated mining event.
	Over two days, there is a conference with 22 speakers, an expo with 90 guests, and seminars. I attended this expo last year as a guest and there were a lot of stalls that were busy with attendees.
	I called one of the companies I knew that exhibited there last year and they said it was a success and gave me some tips.
	There may be an opportunity to present or hold a seminar on the technology and safety issues.
Target market	Attendees: engineers, mine managers, site superintendents, HSE managers, exploration managers and operations managers
	Guest numbers: 20 000 guests over two days
Competitors	90+ other exhibitions. Not clear whether there are any direct competitors until the full list is released
Feasibility	Booth: $4700
	Graphic design: $2000
	Stand set-up and printing: $1500 Attendance: two staff, two days

Investigation into the WA Mining Expo	Findings
Implementation	• Register for a booth • Enquire about the possibility of speaking or holding a seminar on water safety • Engage a graphic designer to produce materials to hand out on the day, including backdrop printing • Inform contacts that I will be exhibiting • Collect business cards or contacts on the day to follow-up • Follow-up with contacts
Goals	Collect contact info for at least 30 people who would be decision-makers for my products

There are a few things that Ashley would need to consider if he was going to choose this marketing channel. Firstly, the investment is large, and he would need to ensure his goals line up with this cost to ensure he can deliver a return on the investment.

Secondly, this kind of investment represents almost all of Ashley's marketing budget for the year, which means he is putting all of his eggs in one basket. In exchange for 30 warm leads, he may find there are other marketing channels that are more affordable that can do the same thing.

Similarly, Ashley could attend the event as a guest and target the same outcomes. Undertaking this exercise helps Ashley see what is possible with marketing, and will also help him make a decision about where to spend his budget. It encourages research and critical thinking and marries up goals with action, which will most likely lead to better results than if he made the decision on a whim.

Focus

After you have completed your investigation, I recommend choosing just one marketing channel (the one that meets your goal criteria) and excluding all the others. This is the marketing channel you are going to implement and focus on for the next 90 days.

Why 90 days?

My 90-day rule is based on the time it takes to fully implement a marketing channel and be able to determine whether it is working to meet your goals or not.

This rule is based on years of implementing everything from SEO campaigns to social ads to proactive business-development strategies. Anything less than 90 days does not give you enough time to solemnly swear that you have tweaked, tested, refined and pushed the limits of the marketing channel you have chosen until it delivers results. Too many business owners give up too soon when a channel is not delivering outcomes. Ensure you have exhausted all options and given it 105 per cent, and at the end of the 90 days your task will be to decide whether to keep it or ditch it.

If you are hitting your goals, gaining traction and managing this channel well, you can keep it. You can also begin the process of choosing another focus for the next 90 days.

If you are not hitting your goals, you need to ditch it. Swiftly. And without hesitation.

Over time, you may find you have ditched more channels than you have kept, but this is an essential part of growth and an important tuning mechanism for any business. Plus you'll have the confidence to say, 'This did not work for my business', without any doubts that you did not give it a good enough go.

Messages and channels

So you've chosen your marketing channel focus for the next 90 days. And now you're wondering what you should put on that channel.

Do you engage a marketing agency, graphic designer, copywriter, programmer or strategist? Each of these functions is going to rely on you to assemble the marketing campaign that is projected on the materials you are putting in front of your audience.

What I mean by this is, if Ashley is creating a brochure for his trade show, what is the message he would like communicated on his brochure to ensure he hits his goals? If he is looking into running LinkedIn advertising, what should his text and image include to make the most of it?

I believe wholeheartedly that getting your marketing message right on your marketing channel is just as important as having the right channels in the first place. Your presence is not enough when you are competing for attention, vying for clicks and trying to set yourself apart from your competitors.

How do I convince them to take action?

For a business like Ashley's, creating a powerful marketing message could have been the difference between success and failure in every conversation he had. But because he was so involved in the intricacies of his business and the technology that he had spent years creating, it was hard for him to create a high-level message that connected with the most number of people.

Creating the marketing message for your marketing channels involves clarity about what you sell and how it solves problems. If customers are confused about what you offer, they will look past you for someone who can say it clearly. To create a marketing message focus effectively, you must truly believe in the following three statements.

First, simple does not mean simplistic. If you set out to explain your company in a simple way, that does not mean you are doing injustice to the superiority and complexities that go into making your product great.

Second, there will be sacrifices. Your products and services do so many things, and creating focus in your marketing message will mean you can't describe them all at once. Trust me when I tell you that saying one thing clearly and simply will be enough to bring someone in closer so that they can learn the rest.

Lastly, there is a difference between knowing how to do something and being known for something. If that makes your head spin, basically what I mean is that you want someone to think of you as soon as they think of the product or service you sell. For example, when you think of smartphones you think of Apple — it's what they are known for. Google knows how to make smartphones, but it isn't what they are known for.

To create your marketing message, you must define a problem that your customers have and explain how you solve it. You must talk about it over and over in the same language, making it crystal clear what it is your company offers. Most companies are too vague and offer 23 things at once that a customer might want. It's confusing.

The king of marketing message simplicity is Donald Miller. In his book *Building a Story Brand,* he breaks down the company message into a very simple statement that satisfies his hypothesis that consumers only have a certain amount of brain calories they are willing to sacrifice each time they come into contact with a new business. If they use them up before getting to the point, they become bored and move onto the next thing. Consumers want to be able to quickly evaluate whether your company solves their problem. If it does, they will investigate further. But identifying the right problem is the key, and it is harder than it might seem.

Your customers have a problem

Recently, I swapped banks.

A new bank lured me away from a bigger competitor, with whom I had been with for many, many years. How? By understanding me at a deeper level than their competitor did.

Let me explain. I have the obvious, surface-level problem that I need somewhere to safely store my money. Most people do. And most banks will tell you that they can help. What this new bank did was offer to solve a deeper problem that I had: I wanted to feel in *control* of my money. I wanted to know where it was going, and I wanted to feel like I was doing the best job of managing it.

While driving, I saw a billboard for my (future) new bank that read, 'Gain total control of your money', accompanied by their app with spending breakdown graphs, easy-to-read categories and a fun interface. This was the marketing message that led to my change of banks. They understood what my deeper problem was beyond just needing a place to store my money.

Customers buy products from you to solve a problem below the surface. They may not even realise they have this problem, but if we can identify that frustration, put it into words and offer to resolve it, something special happens and we bond with the customer.

For example, a company that sells smoke alarms is solving the surface-level problem that the customer does not have a smoke alarm to alert them of a fire. But customers buy smoke alarms because they need to be alerted to a fire to protect their family before it is too late. Identifying your customers' deeper problems and articulating them clearly in your marketing message will further their interest in the story you are telling. It will make them want to investigate and purchase.

Creating your marketing message

To begin crafting your marketing message, you need to take the time to completely understand what problems your customers are facing and how your products are the solution. In the words of Donald Miller, 'People trust those who understand them, and they trust brands that understand them too.' Showing customers that you understand their problems and that you can solve them is the key to crafting marketing messages that turn your marketing channels into successful goal deliverers.

Exercise: Marketing Message

Time required: 1 hour

Stakeholders: Leadership team, marketing professionals, team members

Equipment: Whiteboard, markers

Set-up: Create a three-column table like the one here:

Surface problems	Deeper problems	Success

Method

1. Brainstorm: Your customers are likely facing problems that require your solution. These problems are both surface level and deeper. Start by filling in the first two columns to identify the two categories of problems your customers face.

2. Solve for success: What does success look like when you solve those problems for customers? What is the outcome that your product achieves? In the earlier

example, the problems not having a smoke alarm carry are solved by the success of being alerted if there is a fire. You are solving their concerns by demonstrating success. (Be careful not to confuse the features of your product with the outcome of your product.)

3. Conclude: Tie your deeper problems and your success message together to create a marketing message to use on your different marketing channels.

Marketing message examples

Here are some examples of marketing problems, successes and messages that may inspire the creation of your own targeted message.

SMOKE ALARMS

This company sells smoke alarms for residential homes.

Surface problems	Deeper problems	Success
<ul><li>I do not have a smoke alarm.</li><li>I need to be alerted if there is a fire.</li></ul>	<ul><li>I need to protect my family from danger.</li><li>I want the best chance of survival if there is a fire.</li><li>I do not have peace of mind at the moment.</li></ul>	<ul><li>Family safety is achieved.</li><li>Peace of mind is secured.</li></ul>
Marketing message	We sell reliable smoke alarms so that you and your family always have peace of mind.	

GYROSCOPIC STABILISERS

This company sells equipment that stops boats rocking. If they were to narrow down their target market to boat owners:

Surface problems	Deeper problems	Success
• My boat rocks. • Being on the boat makes me seasick. • I cannot go out in rough weather.	• I want everyone aboard my boat to have a pleasant time. • I can't explore the locations that I want to. • If the weather suddenly changes, the boat ride will be very uncomfortable.	• All days are good boating days. • No one suffers sea sickness. • Comfort on board is achieved.
Marketing message	Stop your boat from rocking so that you and your guests enjoy every minute on board.	

FURNITURE STAGERS

This company lends and sets up furniture for real estate companies for home open viewings.

Surface problems	Deeper problems	Success
• We need to sell this house. • The house does not look its best without furniture, which lowers the chances it will sell. • We need furniture quickly.	• If we do not sell this house, we will be letting our customers down. • We don't know anything about setting up furniture to sell a house. • We may miss the perfect buyer if the house doesn't feel like a home.	• There is furniture in the house that suits it well and shows off its features. • The house is sold quickly, and clients are impressed. • No hassle and no stress for the client.
Marketing message	Show off your properties with our hassle-free furniture hiring and styling service. A guaranteed way to sell your homes faster.	

WATER-COOLING SYSTEMS

Ashley's business sells equipment that cools down potable water in hot climates.

Surface problems	Deeper problems	Success
• Water coming out of the taps is too hot. • We can't access cold water on site quickly. • Hot water poses a safety risk when used in safety equipment. • Bacteria grows when water is always hot.	• Not having access to cold water makes living conditions hard. • We can't guarantee the safety of our employees if essential equipment doesn't work. • Staff may get sick because of water bacteria.	• We know all our safety equipment works when it is required. • Staff and residents are able to access cold water when they need it for their wellbeing and comfort. • Water can be used for all purposes at all times without risk.
Marketing message	We support the mining industry with chilled water technologies that improve the productivity, safety and comfort of employees working in hot environments.	

What you may notice in these examples is that we haven't mentioned much about the actual products and services that these companies sell. This is the key to creating a good marketing message: if you can identify and promise to solve a problem, the viewer will be enticed enough to click and learn more.

The Customer is the hero, not you

An essential element of your marketing message is to ensure you are positioning the Customer, rather than your business, as the hero of the story.

It sounds like an obvious one, but often businesses position themselves as the hero of the story — subconsciously putting their Customers in the back seat. While there is a time and a place for articulating why someone should choose you over your competitors (your years of experience, your awards, etc.), the more important aspect of your message is showing a Customer how they, the hero, can solve all their problems with your assistance.

The best example I've seen of this in the real world was on a bus stop advertisement near my home. It was a big advertisement for yoghurt.

The ad featured a picture of a couple outside a dairy farm. It read, 'This is our favourite yoghurt yet. And we know yoghurt.' A subtitle explained that the yoghurt company was 60 years old and that these two people were the owners of the company.

What the advertisement was trying to convey was authority and expertise; however, what was lacking was how this authority and expertise directly impacted upon the Customer's life. Nothing about it made me, potential yoghurt consumer, feel like the hero at all. In fact, it made me feel less connected to the company.

What this company could have done was shown a family that looked similar to their primary target market, all sitting around the kitchen table, with a caption that read, 'This is your most loved yoghurt yet. Guaranteed to please everyone in the family.'

This kind of caption and wording talks to a few deep problems:

- finding food for the whole family is hard

- kids are fussy eaters

- I never prioritise myself when buying food items for the family

- buying new foods we haven't tried before is a risk.

Have a think about whether you would buy from the first advertisement or the second.

Once you are aware of brands positioning themselves (instead of the Customer) as the hero, you will start to see it everywhere. Do a quick stocktake of marketing you are currently running or have done in the past to see if you are on the right track. If not, make some quick tweaks to your messaging and try again. You may find even small changes make a big difference.

Getting the message right

Over the 90 days you are testing your marketing channel, it is important to experiment with different marketing creative and messages. Just like you are going to work your way through different marketing channels to identify which ones work, it is important to vary the marketing messaging you are using to connect with the right Customers.

Some channels may allow you to create experiments and run multiple creative messaging at once. This is the best way to get immediate answers to whether you are on track.

Actions: What are my next steps?

You've chosen your marketing channel and your marketing message, and the next important part is to take action. So many marketing plans remain unexecuted and forgotten. But not yours!

Action is more important than the plan itself. And now we have a plan, we need to bring it to life.

Using the implementation plan you fleshed out in your marketing channel experiment, begin breaking down the tasks using the following template. You should try and keep the tasks volume small so that you aren't overwhelmed with the number of them, but instead feel like there is a clear and concise plan of action.

Action plan example

Task	Register for a booth
Due date	12 March
Purpose	Registering for a booth locks in my spot at the expo
Outcome	Registration locked in; information provided to me
Tools	◆ Form requirements ◆ Business details ◆ Decision made on booth size
Sub-actions	◆ Fill in form on WA Mining Expo website ◆ Create follow-up reminder if I haven't heard back by end of week ◆ Notify bookkeeper of upcoming credit card payment and purpose ◆ Block out dates in the calendar for expo

Task	Lock in speaker spot
Due date	5 May
Purpose	Exhibitor stands may be ignored; seek opportunity to speak in front of captivated listeners about key expertise topic that can add value
Outcome	Booked in for a 30-minute seminar on water safety on site
Tools	• Keynote presentation brief idea(s) • Speaking reel • Contact email address
Sub-actions	• Find relevant event person in charge of booking speakers • Call and find out more information about who is booked and why • Send through keynote presentation ideas and speaking reel • Create follow-up date in calendar if haven't heard back • Connect on LinkedIn with person • Schedule posts to go out that sample expertise topic

Task	Engage graphic designer to produce materials to hand out on the day, including backdrop printing
Due date	10 May
Purpose	Graphic designer is required to produce the materials we need to hand out to strangers at the expo
Outcome	Everyone leaves with a brochure and impression about our company
Tools	• Brochure and backdrop examples that we like
Sub-actions	• Create list of brochures and backdrops we like the design of • Create a draft layout of each using our new messaging • Contact graphic designer for quotes • Pay deposit

Task	Inform contacts that we will be exhibiting
Due date	20 June
Purpose	Bring traffic and referrals to our booth
Outcome	Lots of foot traffic at our stand and referrals from people who are fans of ours; also re-engagement in conversations that went cold
Tools	♦ LinkedIn ♦ Email
Sub-actions	♦ Create social media posts to announce event ♦ Create list of all cold leads ♦ Draft email to send to all cold leads using new messaging ♦ Reach out to any potential leads or other contacts through LinkedIn messenger to advise of event attendance ♦ Try and arrange meetings at or around the expo with all contacts

Task	Create daily checklist for event
Due date	15 July
Purpose	Ensure we make the most of the expo
Outcome	Every stranger we meet visits our website and gets in touch with us
Tools	♦ Clipboard ♦ Checklist
Sub-actions	♦ Conduct brainstorming session with staff about the event and what we want to get out of it ♦ Brainstorm initiatives to get contact info off traffic ♦ Create checklist that includes KPIs for the day ♦ Create follow-up plan after event ends

Exercise: Action plan

Time required: 2 hours

Stakeholders: Leadership team

Equipment: Paper or online document, calendar, whiteboard

Set-up: Create a blank document with a two column by six row table:

Task	The task in question
Due date	The date it is due
Purpose	Why the task is important
Outcome	What do I want the outcome of this task to be?
Tools	What do I need to get this task done?
Sub-actions	Any specific sub-actions that need to occur

Method

1. Task expansion: Flesh out the tasks required to set up and test your marketing channel. Use the template to collect the information required to get the tasks done. Aim to be concise so that you can bring others onto the same page quickly if you need support bringing the tasks to life.

2. Dates and progress: Use the task names to create a high-level flow of when you are going to get tasks done and who is responsible for doing them.

3. Execution: Execute the tasks according to the plan and adjust subsequent tasks in response, if required.

Did it work?

An important thing to consider as you near the end of your 90-day experiment is, 'did it work?' To answer this question, you are going to need to ensure you are very clear on the goals you set out to achieve and how you are measuring your progress.

For the trade show example, it might be as easy as collecting and counting business cards. However, for more technical marketing channels, it may be harder to track your performance over time without a good grip on your data. You may seek help from a marketing support such as a consultant or an expert who can line your goals up with data so that you can make sure you aren't guessing when it comes to the end of the 90-day period.

And remember, if it doesn't look promising, ditch it. Regardless of how much money, effort or time you have put into trying it, if it is not meeting your goals or doesn't look like it is going to meet your goals, it has to be sacrificed. Too many businesses lock themselves into a marketing channel or plan that is just not working.

This reluctance to abandon a strategy is a natural human reaction that is triggered by discomfort when new evidence or facts clash with something we believe in. Sometimes business owners — and even entire companies — don't want to lose the resources they have already invested, and we don't want to appear inconsistent.

However, if it is working, great! You can continue with it, invest more time or effort into it, or add another marketing channel to the mix by choosing your next focus from your earlier investigation.

I recommend undertaking the Bullseye exercise a few times a year to make sure you are on top of any new channels, trends or information when it comes to attracting Strangers.

So what happened to the trade show, and did Ashley decide to keep this channel or ditch it?

With such a big investment, it was integral that Ashley focused on making the most out of this marketing channel. Not only did it take up most of his budget for the year, but it was not an event that came around often: it was a one-shot activity.

With the booth set-up, brochures printed and a list of potential targets, Ashley and his team spent the two days at the conference meeting as many people as they possibly could. They focused on the mantra to 'keep it simple', practicing their marketing message to everyone they met and remembering that this conversation was just the first of many steps in the customer journey. They didn't have to turn someone from a Stranger to a Lead just in one ten-minute conversation.

By the end of the conference, Ashley and his team had 42 potential leads to follow up. They followed their action plan and waited two days to follow up on the leads, they crafted the perfect introduction on LinkedIn, sent through a link to their website and arranged further coffee catch ups in the hopes all these people would become official Leads for the business. And many of them did!

Although his proposals to speak at the conference weren't accepted this time, Ashley spent time attending other presentations to learn more about how to craft the kind of presentation that the organisers were looking for. He also arranged to meet up with two of the presenters to ask them about the presenting process and applying for a speaker spot. Next year might be his year!

This method worked out for Ashley, but only because he gave the entire process deliberation and consideration, taking his time to ensure he could give every action step 105 per cent of his efforts.

Why growth stops

Remember that to feed your marketing system you will need a steady stream of Strangers making their way through to becoming Fans. But without this, growth stops. There are three key reasons I see growth stopping when clients have completed the Bullseye exercise.

1. They go back to a scattered approach of haphazardly choosing marketing channels. Regressing to the 'shiny new thing' marketing approach happens a lot and for a lot of reasons. Maybe you've gotten into a good rhythm with implementing marketing techniques and you want to speed up the process. Maybe you've gotten a tempting offer from a marketing partner or agency. Maybe a competitor has done something you are inspired by. It's easy to get tripped up and to let things fall by the wayside. If you continue to maintain a rhythm for checking in on your marketing, and being structured in the way you investigate opportunities, you won't waste money.

2. Their message has morphed. Over time, it is easy for a marketing message to morph or change with variations in imagery or campaigns. New opinions coming in or advice from other agencies can take you far away from where you started, and it can be easy to think that customers are getting tired of the simple marketing message you started with. So let me remind you what we are doing here at the front of your marketing system: you are attracting *Strangers* to your business. They haven't seen your marketing message before, so although you have come across it a thousand times and it is tempting to change it, hold back! It is still brand new to the people you want to target.

3. They stop paying attention to marketing. When things are going right, it's hard to make the time to focus on marketing to Strangers and innovating the way you reach new people. You're flat out running the business! And the last thing you want is to let your new customers down. I get it. But this is the biggest thing I see stopping growth for our clients: starting something and then forgetting about it. It's not easy, but investing in your marketing is the best energy you will ever devote to your business.

In a nutshell

In this chapter we explored the process required to turn Strangers into Visitors and kickstart your entire marketing system. We discussed the importance of this stage of the customer journey and emphasised the importance of having a strategy that enables you to tackle things with 105 per cent of effort, one at a time.

The ability to achieve a good conversion rate from Stranger to Visitor relies on the harmony of three things: the channel, the message and the action.

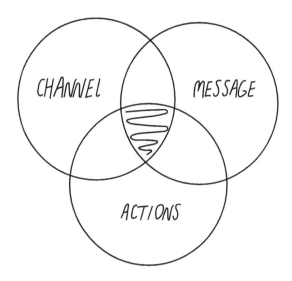

Getting in front of the right people (channel)

Getting in front of the right people is all about analysing all the marketing channels available to your business and brainstorming, investigating and focusing in on one for a set period of time to the exclusion of any other.

☐   Exercise to complete: Bullseye

Convincing them to take action (message)

A clear marketing message that talks to the Stranger's external and internal problems is the thing that will encourage them to take action. Keep it simple, and use it over and over.

☐   Exercise to complete: Marketing Message

Executing it (action)

So many marketing plans remain unexecuted and forgotten. Creating an action plan that focuses on outcomes is essential for success and alignment.

☐   Exercise to complete: Action Plan

FIVE

HOW TO TURN A VISITOR INTO A LEAD

Most businesses have a website. However, a lot of businesses don't have a website that converts Visitors into Leads. What I mean by that is that people who are visiting do not enquire, phone, email or send carrier pigeons to that business. They've found the website somehow through a marketing channel, and then decided not to proceed with becoming a Customer or Fan of that business.

It's quite a common occurrence, and so many businesses don't even realise their website is the thing letting down their entire growth system.

If you're doing well in this space, you can expect between a 3 per cent and 5 per cent conversation rate from your website — so 3 per cent to 5 per cent of the people visiting will enquire and become Leads, either by calling or by submitting an enquiry form. You may be surprised that this number is so low — you may never have even looked at this number before if your website goals haven't been clearly recorded or defined. Either way, to really beat this bottleneck, you want to ensure your conversion rate from Visitor to Lead is above 5 per cent.

As a marketing professional who started out in website development, there are a whole heap of lessons I have learnt over the years about websites and the things that make them ineffective. In my experience, most business owners will fall victim to some of these harsh realities that make their website their bottleneck towards growth.

The price of a website is confusing

Nowadays, building a website can cost your business anywhere from $29 a month all the way up to $30 000, depending on who builds it, how it is built, what is included and the design elements required. It is incredibly confusing for business owners who constantly struggle to compare price and value in such a saturated market.

What you should know: In the overwhelming majority of cases, a website that costs $29 a month and a website that costs $30 000 a month can both achieve the same outcomes with the right ingredients. Being clear on what you want the website to achieve and the ingredients that are going to make it happen will enable you to achieve success regardless of what avenue you go down price-wise.

Websites use up a lot of your marketing budget

Getting a good website can cost a lot of money and therefore take up a good chunk of your marketing budget. This results in a few things: you aren't left with any money for the other marketing activities in your marketing system, you neglect to continue spending money improving your website after it is built, and you put a lot of pressure on it to deliver a good amount of return for your business,

What you should know: If your website is your biggest bottleneck, spending your budget on it will likely pay dividends for your whole marketing system. But you need to keep giving it attention so that it doesn't go stale and lose its effectiveness over time. Consider checking in on your website every quarter.

Your website and marketing channel don't match

As was the case for Ashley in chapter 4, his website did not do as good a job of talking about his products and services as he did in person. This left Visitors confused and unsure about taking the next step.

What you should know: The process of building a website can be very complex and confusing, and it often ends up very far away from the rest of your marketing system. Keeping it simple and remembering its purpose (encouraging people to enquire) ensures it remains effective and consistent.

Building a website is more than just design

Websites need good design, plus conversion-mechanisms, plus clear content. A lot of website developers can create good design and a flashy user experience, but not a lot will combine good design with conversions and clear content. It covers too many disciplines, and many web designers will expect business owners to just send through the content rather than working with them to arrange it on the website to improve conversions.

What you should know: You will need to take control of this — leaving the whole strategy for your website to your website designer will result in ineffectiveness. I've seen it time and time again. Use this chapter to craft a website that really works.

Website technology is complicated

For a small business owner, website technology can seem scary. There are so many ways of developing websites, from DIY platforms through to coded-from-scratch server platforms. This makes it a daunting marketing mechanism for individuals wanting to get more of a grip on what happens in the background, and website developers often won't divulge their secrets

What you should know: Ensure you take the time to learn a bit about how your website was built and is managed so that you can update it yourself if you need to. The knowledge will never go wasted, and you will feel more comfortable about investing money into it if you know how it works.

Your website tries to talk to everyone

Most businesses are using an 'umbrella' website to cover-off all their primary, secondary and subsequent markets. This means the unique selling points and marketing messages are spread far and wide and end up being generic rather than talking directly to someone in a way that spurs action.

What you should know: Talking to one group well is always better than doing a half-hearted job of talking to many. It's tricky, but it will pay dividends.

Website data is never tracked or used

What even is channel? Or source? Clicks? Sessions? Time on page? Events? Goals? Website analytics can often be too overwhelming for small business owners to dive into when it comes to their website, let alone make any sort of conclusion about their performance. Unless you're tracking goals effectively, it is almost impossible to know if your website is doing its job of converting Leads into Visitors.

What you should know: If you are very clear on what information you want from your website (e.g. how many Leads it is delivering), you can seek the help you need to get that answer. Start with your website developer or hosting platform, talk to them about how you get this answer and follow the trail until that information is flowing regularly.

Someone will always have a better-looking website

How your website looks will always be a number one focus for most business owners. You want it to look the best — better than competitors, better than a previous website you had. When something looks visually appealing, it releases dopamine, so it is no surprise that website design is important.

What you should know: Website design is important, but remember: looks are subjective. How it looks doesn't mean anything if it doesn't say the right things or convince people to take action. There will always be a shiny new website design trend and it is easy to get trapped in design to your detriment.

Linda's bottleneck

These website truths were all too real for small-business owner Linda, who I met when her business had hit a growth plateau. Linda is a specialist speech pathologist who works with children who have complex conditions, such as cognitive-communication disorders. Linda's practice began as just her, but over the last few years she has expanded her business to include another practitioner, and they wanted to expand their services to include children with a wider range of speech disorders in a wider variety of locations across rural WA.

When I first met Linda, I was blown away by the scope of her knowledge and her 'why' behind what she did. Many of the children she worked with had been misdiagnosed or unable to receive or finance treatment, leaving them behind other children and struggling with other behavioural disorders.

Linda was working hard to educate support coordinators, family planners, educators and child health workers to identify speech disorders better for early intervention. She also had specialist training in cognitive-communication disorders, which were often the result of trauma or in utero conditions, and she wanted to ensure children with this diagnosis were offered specialist services rather than generic speech pathology.

However, despite all her work, all her contacts and the advocating she had done, she had not received an increase in referrals for at least 12 months. With the same number of referrals, but an increased amount of work happening to attract Strangers, Linda was really keen to investigate how she could reach the growth goals she had set for her practice and what she was missing.

Linda's website

Linda's website for her practice was very simple and included only a few pages. She had it assembled by a graphic designer when she first began her practice three years ago, and hadn't done a lot of work examining why or how it could be impacting her business growth. At first glance, it was clear and simple. However, it was easy to see the discrepancies between the way she explained her business, her goals and her clients to me, and the actual website that existed online.

Diving into her website analytics told a similar story. Linda's website was getting a lot of direct hits from a lot of different users. But the number of people calling or enquiring was low. Her conversion rate was less than 1 per cent.

Linda wasn't aware of this at all, but her efforts out in the market building relationships were actually working well! It was using her website as an effective marketing tool to turn those Visitors into Leads that was the issue. Linda's website looked good, and functioned well, but it was lacking a few key things that, once implemented, began to completely transform her business.

Fast forward a few years, and Linda's business (along with her website) is completely different. Linda now has six employees, more locations across WA and more referrals than she can handle.

So what exactly did she do?

Linda started by implementing the 7 essential Ss into her website. These are seven simple, but essential, elements that every website needs to convert at 5 per cent or above, and ensure all your efforts to attract Strangers have the best chance of converting them into a Lead for your business.

It wasn't an expensive process, and there wasn't a complete website redesign. Instead, it was a case of truly understanding what ingredients in her website were required to make an impact and then watching those changes make a difference.

The 7 essential Ss for a high-performing website

Not all websites perform the same, but the ones that do perform well have a lot of things in common that have nothing to do with the products or services they sell. These simple website must-haves can make a huge difference to the overall performance of your site, and can contribute to more Visitors becoming the Leads that will eventually grow your business.

Linda's website was not a bad website by any means. She worked with a freelance website designer who had a specialty in design, which meant that the website looked nice. It had a nice logo, headers, stock images with a bit of colour overlayed, text on each page and was mobile responsive. The people Lauren showed the site to — her husband, her friends, her colleagues — all said the site looked great. However, they already knew what her services were and what her unique selling point was. To me, however, I wasn't sure what she was selling, what made her business unique, how to get in touch with her or even what kinds of people she was marketing to. And the same thing was likely occurring to all the Strangers she was trying to attract.

And it wasn't until she was able to implement the 7 essential Ss that things began to change.

1. The Six-second impression

My number one rule for websites is this: If you don't understand what a company sells or how to get it within six seconds or less, then it's never going to happen.

Why? Because, as we learnt in chapter 2, consumers are drawn away from confusion and towards clarity.

Your intention isn't to create a confusing website, but companies can slip into this trap by over-explaining their products, trying to fit in as much information as they can or just not knowing how to clearly structure what it is that they sell. Other pitfalls include using taglines or messaging that is too complex or clever, or employing design elements that distract from the clarity of your message.

It's reported that 75 per cent of consumers admit to making judgements about a company's credibility based on the company's website, so it is absolutely essential that you land those six seconds.

As soon as your website loads, everything on that first loading screen needs to cover these three non-negotiables to ensure your six-second impression is powerful:

◆   what problem you solve

◆   what you sell

◆   how to get it.

And it needs to make sense for everyone, not just for you and people who know your business, but for complete strangers. Don't automatically assume people know what you are talking about: you will never offend someone knowledgeable by spelling out a concept in simple terms.

For Linda's business, this was her six-second impression.

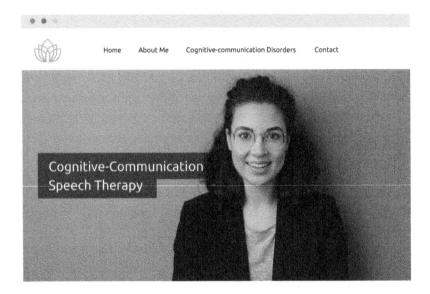

Straight away, it is unclear what Linda sells and how someone can get in touch with her. Although it's visually appealing, the first impression of her website is confusing, especially for her target market who are looking for a good speech pathologist to support a participant or loved one. Fortunately, with a few small edits this was easy to solve, and it will be easy for you to solve too.

For Linda's website, we implemented the following changes:

- fleshed out her menu to include all of her services

- updated her main above-the-fold message to clearly state what she does

- chose two call-to-action messages to make it easier for both her target markets to take the next steps to working with her

- updated the image on the website to include a picture of success rather than a picture of herself.

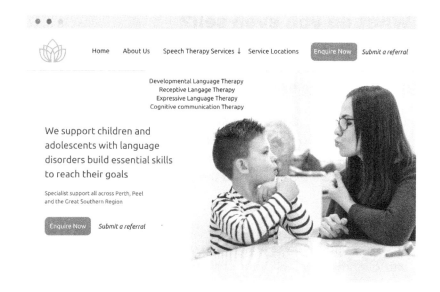

Making these small changes completely changes the impression of her website. It focuses on the customer, quickly articulates what it is she does and what she offers, and it has a clear next step for anyone interested.

Let's dive into those in more detail.

2. A clear Sitemap

Connected to the first 'S' of website success, but still its own very important ingredient in a successful website, is the sitemap. The sitemap of your website dictates the pages and the hierarchy of your content so that it can be digested in a clear and simple way.

Clarity on what you sell and who you sell it to is not only essential for your website, but is an essential exercise for your entire business.

What do you even sell?

Would it surprise you to hear that at least 60 per cent of the clients we meet don't have a clear understanding of what they sell and who they sell it to?

It sounds crazy, but over time, as businesses grow and pivot, it can become really cloudy about what exactly it is that they sell. Perhaps they've identified a new market or a new product, or else changed the structure of their offering over time.

Now is as good a time as any to ensure you have your products and markets mapped in a way that creates clarity and alignment for all your stakeholders, whether they be clients, staff or other suppliers.

Here's how you do it:

The Hierarchy

This method is ideal for a business with a complex spread of products that are designed for one broad market. Start by mapping out your main product categories. Use hierarchies to expand further product subcategories below this until you have your entire product spread mapped.

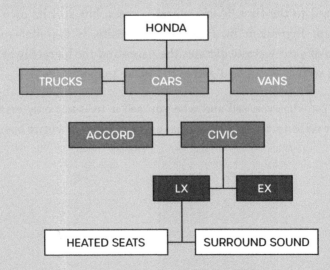

The Matrix

This method is ideal for businesses with multiple markets and products. Start by filling in one product for one market in the starting square. Then expand out the 'blocks' to the right or the left depending on whether you:

+ offer that same product to a second unique market

+ have introduced a unique product to the first market.

+ Eventually, you will have a spread of products and markets in your commercial model that give clarity to how you sell your products.

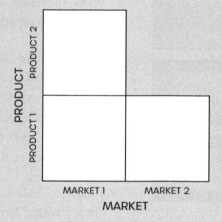

This exercise often helps businesses structure their website (and their business). It ensures you have clarity around what you sell and who you sell it to in a simple but powerful way that gives a big-picture overview to the Visitors who want a quick, six-second impression of your company.

For Linda's business, she concluded that she was saying yes to a lot of different clients across different markets and age groups. This is common for businesses starting out, but it blurs the lines between 'what you know how to do' and 'what you are known for'. It meant

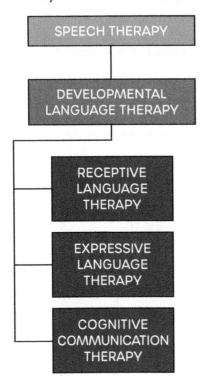

that she was saying yes to working with adults, kids and teenagers, as well as on speech disorders from fluency and articulation through to complex language disorders. It made it hard for people to refer her business, and it also made it hard to create a website that explained everything.

Together, we identified that she wanted to 'be known' for supporting children and adolescents with language disorders, and this was how she mapped out her products and services.

This changed her website menu quite a bit, and it now looks like this:

- Home

- About Us

- Speech Therapy Services

  - Developmental Language Therapy

  - Receptive Language Therapy

  - Expressive Language Therapy

  - Cognitive Communication Therapy

- Service Locations

- Enquire Now

- Submit a referral

Her original sitemap (Home; About Me; Cognitive-communication Disorders; Contact) covered off a lot of basics, but it lacked a full breakdown of her services, which her target market was looking for after meeting her. She also identified that a lot of people were coming to her site to just look for a place to submit a referral, so she ensured it was front and centre on her new sitemap.

For your business, it is similarly important that you create a website menu that mimics your product or service offering in a clear and logical way.

BROWSERS AND LOGICIANS

In my experience, most websites will have two distinct kinds of Visitors: Browsers and Logicians. Browsers will make their way down your home page, clicking links, bouncing from page to page until they make a decision. Logicians will work their way from the left to the right of your menu. They will scroll down a page, scroll back up and proceed to the next one, not wanting to miss any information.

This means that you have to cater for both, and ensure you are presenting your information as clearly and concisely as possible so that every single Visitor that comes to your website has the best chance of getting in touch.

Over time, as your business evolves, you should re-examine your website menu and ensure it still aligns with your actual business, the products/services you offer and how you introduce it to Strangers.

3. Next Steps: what are they?

Around 70 per cent of small business websites lack a call to action (you may have seen it referred to as CTA) on their homepage. A call to action is the button on your website that helps someone take the next step, whether that be to contact your business, start a free trial, download something etc.

Without it, customers are left wandering around in circles trying to work out how to engage your business to solve their problems. We have three key rules for a good call to action:

1. Calls to action should feature action-orientated words that encourage users to take the next step, such as 'take this course', 'book an event', 'get a quote' or 'shop now'.

2. The button needs to stand out. Generally speaking, bright green and orange buttons perform better than any other, but you do want to make sure it suits your branding on your website. It should also be large, and the text should be very legible. This includes displaying it on the website menu.

3. Repeat your buttons again and again throughout the page to ensure that, not only is it clear what you want the Visitor to do, but you also cater for both Browsers and Logicians and give them a place to take the next step regardless of where they are in their journey.

Take a moment to examine your website and the kind of buttons you currently display.

For Linda's original site, she had a simple 'Contact' menu item acting as her call to action. She wanted everyone to contact her company after visiting her website. Seems simple enough. Beyond the reality that not many people were drawn to the small item on the menu, she further identified that her target market wanted to do more than 'contact'. They wanted to 'submit a referral', and they wanted to do it quickly. We expanded her website to include two call-to-action buttons. One that said, 'Enquire now' and one that said, 'Submit a referral'.

With 'Enquire now' being the primary button (e.g. it was in the brightest, boldest colour next to 'Submit a referral'), it was easy for someone to spot their next step, but they also had the more direct option of submitting a referral.

Enquire Now   *Submit a referral*

We repeated these buttons throughout the website so that it was consistently clear that the next steps to working with her company were one of those two things.

Exercise: Your six-second impression

Time required: 10 minutes

Stakeholders: Leadership team, marketing professionals

Equipment: Template below, pen and paper

Setup: Use this template to plan your six-second impression.

Method

Now that we've covered the first three essentials for a high-performing website, it's your turn to evaluate how well your website is working for your business. This template is a simple way of assessing the first six seconds of someone's experience on your website. Consider your answers to the questions in the list and how they apply to your website. Then make a plan for how to implement any changes to improve your customers' experience.

1. What problem do you solve? The section of your website that loads first is what we often call the 'above the fold' message. It is the first text element that loads on a website (outside of the main menu), and it should very clearly explain to the reader how you solve problems. This sentence should check the following boxes:

   ☐ plain language (nothing clever, no insider language)

   ☐ short and sweet

   ☐ clearly explain how you solve a problem *or* clearly explain what it is that you do.

Underneath this sentence you can expand on your point a bit further by summarising what you sell or including additional information about your target market. (For more instructions on this message, jump back to chapter 4 and review the 'Creating your marketing message' section.)

2. What do you sell? Your menu loads first on a website, so it needs to do a good job at explaining what it is that you sell. Whether you choose to utilise a dropdown menu to list your products and services, or have them listed across the top of the menu, it is important your visitors can see what they can buy from you to solve their problems.

3. How do they get it? Stating clearly what a business or customer needs to do to buy your products and services is key. There's no point convincing a Visitor that you can solve their problem if you don't back it up with clear instructions on how to buy it.

4. Solve problems

Your products and services solve a problem. But you need your website to explain to Visitors just how big that problem is for them to be motivated enough to purchase the solution. It's simple psychology, but many small businesses neglect to do this, and it can have an impact on the conversion rate of their website.

The reason for this is that the majority of people visiting your website are unlikely to buy (remember, we said that a *good* conversion rate on a website is around 3 per cent to 5 per cent), and going from a Stranger to a Lead usually takes some deliberation and convincing on your website's part. What better way to convince someone than to really articulate the problems they have now so that the solution seems important. What are the stakes? What happens if they don't buy the solution?

You need to ensure your website articulates that the gap between where the Visitor is today (riddled with problems) and the future they desperately want is really far apart. Opening up that gap between problem and solution only makes someone want it more, and when your product or service is the thing helping them make the journey, then you've won.

Doing this is simple. It's about painting the problem picture before paining the picture of success. Usually, this is done in text, and it should be fairly high up on your website.

An example is this:

> **Tailored Language Therapy can make the world of difference**
>
> When it comes to finding language therapy for a loved one or a client, working with the right provider is essential, and the search can be tedious. The wrong provider can set you back

months, if not years, from reaching simple language and cognitive milestones that will contribute significantly to daily life at school, in the home and in the community.

Text like this opens up that problem-solution gap just a little bit so that the Visitor can identify what the stakes may be if they don't find a solution — and fast.

5. A picture of Success

Conversely to the above, mirroring the problem with success thanks to your products and services is imperative to demonstrating that you can help them get to the outcome they are now desperate for.

You may end the above paragraph with:

> Through our dedicated approach to language therapy, good support is the minimum that we deliver. In fact, we tailor our approach so closely to the goals and desired outcomes of our clients, that therapy sessions are welcomed events that continue to deliver progress when we aren't even there.

Success should also be used in imagery on your website, to paint the picture of what life looks like after someone has purchased your products and services.

Often this needs a little thinking outside the box: success can often be a feeling or a facial expression. The idea of imagery like this originates in a basic psychological principle surrounding likeability. We like things that are similar to us. We can foster liking based on the similarity principle if we claim to have a similar background and interests to the person we want to persuade; for example, 'Our happy customers look just like you' or 'The people in this image are experiencing an emotion like the emotion you want to feel'.

Exercise: Problems and Solutions

Time required: 1 hour

Stakeholders: Leadership team, marketing professionals

Equipment: Pen, paper

Method

1. On your own or in a group, brainstorm a list of all the problems that your target market is currently experiencing. Ensure these are 'internal' problems, and steer clear from literal wording such as: 'My customer does not have a smoke alarm'. Instead, the problem would be: 'My customer is not going to be alerted if there is a fire' or 'My customer's life is at risk if there is a fire'.

2. Assemble some of these problems in a paragraph for your website. You can use bullet points to cover off multiple problems or else construct a full paragraph around a key issue.

3. Now brainstorm what success looks like for that same target market. Things like: 'Peace of mind that the family will be safe'.

4. Assemble the mirror wording to the problem statement by concluding the first paragraph with how your company delivers success.

5. Find imagery that represents your target market's idea of success to use on your website. Try to capture key target markets displaying emotions or expressions that resemble those you want your customers to experience. You can use stock image websites to find these or else engage a photographer.

6. Sidekick mode: You're not the hero

In chapter 4, I discussed positioning your customer as the hero. If you're not onto that bottleneck yet, I'll give you a quick rundown.

Many businesses start their copy and messaging with the word 'we'. 'We are great', 'we sell this', 'we do that'. It makes the entire narrative about the company when the focus should be about their customer. So many websites do this without realising and it can significantly contribute to a poor conversion rate.

Instead of leading with you and making the website about why your business is great, focus on what you provide to your customer and how you make their life better.

Rather than:

'We are leading language disorder therapists in WA.'

Try:

'We support children and adolescents with language disorders build essential skills to reach their goals.'

Choosing the second option over the first connects with Visitors more; however, it opens you up to a creative challenge: proving the first statement is true without having to say it. This means walking the walk, not just talking the talk. Why are you the leading language therapy company?

Is it your size? Your success rate? Your accreditations? Combined knowledge?

All of these are known as 'authority indicators', and they are the formal backup that give Visitors the confidence they are looking for to get in touch. Yes, anyone can promise success, but why are you the one they should trust over others?

Building out the following on your website is essential, and if you do it in a balanced way, it will position you as the very qualified sidekick in someone else's story:

- testimonials

- accreditations

- years in business

- size of team

- combined knowledge

- awards and achievements

- projects and portfolio

- reviews.

Exercise: Authority Indicators

Time required: 1 hour

Stakeholders: Leadership team, marketing professionals

Equipment: Pen, paper

Method

1. Brainstorm what makes your business the best. What are your authority indicators that can back up bold statements like, 'you should pick us over others'?

2. Collect evidence for them.

3. Display them on your website.

7. Soft leads

So, someone has visited your website, but they aren't quite ready to enquire or buy from you yet. They are somewhat interested because they visited your website in the first place, but for some reason they aren't ready to take the next step. They really only have one choice now: to leave.

Hopefully they come back later …

If only there was something in between enquiring and leaving that adds value and keeps you in contact with that visitor until they are ready to become an official Lead.

Fortunately, there is!

And this is what marketing professionals call a 'soft lead'. This is an email address you have collected in your database from Visitors not ready to buy yet, and the conversion rate from Visitor to soft lead can often be as high as 40 per cent.

Collecting them is easy. All you need to do is create something really valuable that someone is willing to exchange their email for, such as a video, a PDF download or a free webinar.

You may be familiar with this technique, and may have handed over your own information before for a transaction. It is likely you then received emails from that company, and may have even purchased from them.

The reason soft leads are an integral part of any website is that once you have an email address, you can build a relationship and nurture that soft lead until they are ready to become a Lead or even a Customer. All with very little effort.

When you offer something valuable in exchange for something as simple as an email address, it can seem like a no-brainer to the customer, and it should be a no-brainer for you. Here's why.

CONSTANT CONTACT

The attention span of a human means your customers have likely forgotten all about you weeks, if not days, after they visited your website. Even if a soft lead doesn't covert right away, you have a number of chances to encourage them once you have their email.

PREVIEW YOUR WORTH

Something valuable in exchange for an email is often the best way of giving future Customers a preview of the value you can add. Whether that is a PDF that gives away knowledge or a software trial, anything you can do that helps bridge the gap, even slightly, between a Customer's problem and their future success is a win.

MORE TIME

A support coordinator downloaded a PDF from Linda's website entitled, 'The difference between receptive and expressive language delays and how you can identify both'. They then received a series of follow-up emails that included a research article, a support structure example, a case study from a therapy structure overseas, a behind-the-scenes image and a referrals process map. All this information was available on the website, but it's unlikely that it has been discovered by every visitor.

By taking the time to send this information through in a way that pitched it as extra value, Linda was able to build a seemingly closer relationship with this Visitor than she would have if they just visited the website alone.

WARMER THAN BEFORE

After nurturing a soft lead over time, the likelihood they will become a Lead and then a Customer is much greater than if they were a Visitor sending an enquiry. They feel invested now, they have been given value, and they are likely to reciprocate. This means that it's going to be easier to turn them into a Customer and, therefore, your business will have a leg up with very little work.

To introduce soft leads effectively, it is important you focus on value before anything else. The initial offer needs to be almost too good to refuse (This much value for free? What!?), and the subsequent emails need to have subject titles so good they are opened every time. Do not use these emails as an excuse to broadcast sales pitches or offers. Building a relationship with Leads is all about adding value.

Exercise: Soft Leads

Time required: 4 hours

Stakeholders: Leadership team, marketing professionals

Equipment: Pen, paper, computer

Method

1. Review the problems your customers are facing and identify ways to help them on their journey in small, bite-sized chunks.

2. Create an asset that delivers that value. Some ideas are a free:

   - ebook/PDF/case study delivered to their inbox

   - video series

   - webinar

- worksheet or workbook

- trial

- consultation call.

3. Create a nurture email series to send after the asset is downloaded. Aim for three to six emails, with a call to action at the end of each.

4. Use a bulk-email-sending software to execute the system and the help of a technical professional, if required.

Why people stop marketing here

An interesting business paradox that plagues the small business industry especially, is the absence of a marketing strategy beyond the delivery of 'leads'. Once a business has converted a Stranger to a Lead, marketing has done its job, apparently, and so says almost every marketing agency in Australia.

If your business is still growing, has less than 20 staff and doesn't have an active business development team, it is a mistake to separate marketing and sales for the sake of business growth. In fact, regardless of the size of your organisation, marketing and sales need to be intertwined to ensure that the messaging, the market and the disciplines remain consistent across the entire organisation to reach the goals you set out to achieve.

Zenith Media's Five Commerce Imperatives for Marketers shone a light on a big opportunity for businesses to improve growth. They identified that numerous brands are missing opportunities to drive growth because their marketing and sales teams operate in silos.

As a result, separate sales and marketing teams, often with different objectives and performance indicators, employ different messaging, strategies, platforms, persuasion techniques and information to convert the same Customer on the same journey.

Unfortunately, this disconnect can dramatically reduce the conversion rate in sales. Customers get confused, and this shouldn't happen — not if your organisation views the customer journey as one, and your teams operate as a cohesive unit.

When you get it right, how you turn Leads into Customers becomes another business process that feels organic and easy. It should be delivered consistently every single time, but it also needs a deliberate strategy that is underpinned with a marketing strategy.

In a nutshell

In this chapter we reviewed the reasons most websites aren't working for small business owners. We met Linda, a specialist speech therapist, and used her business as an example to demonstrate the 7 essential Ss of a high-performing website. Perhaps your website has some of these already built in, or you might have an opportunity to make some improvements. The good news is that all of these changes are bite-sized, meaning they don't require a complete overhaul and they will make a lot of difference.

Here they are again:

1. The Six-second impression

If you don't understand what a company sells or how to get it within six seconds or fewer, then it's never going to happen. Your website needs to clearly demonstrate what problem you solve, what you sell and how to get it within the first six seconds of it loading.

2. A clear Sitemap

It is essential that your website has a clear sitemap that is easy to navigate and is reflective of your product or service offering. Using a hierarchy or matrix model is an effective way of examining your offering in the eyes of a Stranger so you can mimic it on your website.

3. Next Steps: what are they?

Around 70 per cent of small business websites lack a call to action on their website. This leaves your visitors wondering what they need to do next. It is essential your call to actions are action-orientated, bright and distinctive, and repeated throughout the site.

☐ Exercise to complete: Your six-second impression

4. Solve problems

Your website needs to not only show that you solve your Visitor's problems, but make sure they know the stakes if they don't solve those problems. This is done through painting the problem in clear, evocative language.

5. A picture of Success

Once you've articulated the problem, your website needs to paint the picture of success by explaining what life looks like once your Customer has solved it. Do this in text and images, explaining how your company will help them take the journey.

☐ Exercise to complete: Problems and Solutions

6. Sidekick mode: You're not the hero

Make your website less about you and more about what you provide to your Customer, and how you make their life better. Then seek out authority indicators to back up why you are the best sidekick on their journey to success.

☐ Exercise to complete: Authority Indicators

7. Soft Leads

If the gap between a Visitor and a Lead is just too great for most of your Visitors to jump in one sitting, you could consider introducing a soft lead status. A soft lead is where you collect an email address from a website visitor in exchange for something valuable, and then nurture them over time until they are ready to buy. Soft leads are a great way of improving your overall conversion rate, especially for products and services that have a higher value.

☐ Exercise to complete: Soft Leads

SIX

HOW TO TURN A LEAD INTO A CUSTOMER

So, here's the really, tangibly important part of your customer journey: generating revenue.

You've attracted them, you've flirted with them, you've dated them and now's the big moment they make a commitment. So, you better put your best foot forward because if they run away, they probably won't ever return.

The bigger your company gets, the more siloed the marketing and sales parts of your business will become. The people who look after marketing are focused on Strangers, the sales team are focused on Customers. They appear as two separate entities, possibly run by two separate teams with two unique sets of KPIs — and this can be a disaster.

I've worked with many organisations where the marketing and sales division are so divided that they don't even agree on the same high-level unique product selling points.

Whilst the actions and the skills required to attract Strangers and convert Leads may seem independent, what the silos create is a disjointed customer experience that can leave a potential buyer confused and disenchanted. Imagine enjoying a convincing Google advertisement, a stunning website and a clear call to action only to be met with a string of unanswered and confusing emails from Amanda on my skirting board quest. It was not only frustrating, but I felt tricked! I really wanted those skirting boards now, and when I couldn't have them, it made me feel angry and like somebody had wasted my time.

So, viewing the entire customer journey as one system is not only going to improve your success rate through a consistent message and delivery, it could quite possibly change the trajectory of your entire business.

Fortunately for small businesses, the ability to view your entire customer journey as one is a lot simpler because, as an owner, it is likely that you frequently check in on all areas of the business. You may even still be responsible for the sales system, personally talking to each Customer and building relationships with them that fuel your revenue.

This was the case for Simon who, if you remember from chapter 3, ran the business development and sales system for his engineering company. When he finally stepped out of that role after five years, sales conversions plunged to an all-time low. They discovered that converting Leads into sales was not as simple as delivering a price to someone who enquired through their website. It was a whole lot more than that.

The 6 fundamentals of converting Leads into Customers

Sales, just like any other process within your business, must be a process that can be replicated, scaled and delivered consistently every time. It is a formula unique to your business that, when implemented, has the absolute best chance of converting every Lead into a Customer.

Some things, however, will be the same for every business. Similar to the principles we employ on a website, converting Leads comes with a checklist of best practices your company will swear by — and they aren't complex or complicated.

The 6 fundamentals of converting Leads into Customers are the steps that small businesses need to have built into their customer journey system to guarantee success. Each one is a non-negotiable, and form the start of a system that you will need to keep perfecting over the life of your business.

1. Effective use of a customer relationship management (CRM) system

In chapter 3, when Simon and Julia took the Bottleneck Quiz, it opened their eyes to the fact that their business was no longer revolving around a handful of key customer relationships that Simon could manage out of his contacts in his phone. It was an entity, and that entity needed to have its own relationship with clients outside of the ones that were nurtured and developed by Simon.

This meant that all the knowledge and history with those clients needed to come out of Simon's head and live within something that belonged to the business. This was essential to enabling the business to grow and scale without Simon, so that anyone could pick up the phone and continue a conversation with a potential Customer as if it were Simon himself.

Imagine how you would feel as a customer if you had a relationship with Simon that suddenly went away. You were used to calling him directly, emailing him any time of the day or night, and then suddenly you're waiting one to two business days for an email response from someone who treats you like a complete stranger. You went from

10/10 service to something that, even though it was still great, felt like rubbish.

Customer relationships management (CRM) systems are the first ingredient in transforming this because they store the knowledge that helps ensure everyone is on the same page when it comes to customer interactions and data. So, even when Simon exits his role completely, his knowledge about his customers can live on and be injected into every interaction a subsequent employee has with customers for years and years to come.

But CRM systems don't just stop there. CRM systems support you in managing enquiries, quoting, and examining data and trends so that your entire sales system can be relatively automatic. You can see where every quote is (aka you won't lose track of anything), every customer response (no more private conversations), and even create automatic communication that adds value or nudges the Lead towards becoming a Customer without your help.

IMPLEMENTING A CRM

Simon handed over his role in sales before any kind of CRM system was implemented. His sales process was managed by responding to emails and phone calls, as well as recording follow-ups and notes in his personal notepad that he carried around.

His newly appointed estimating and sales team followed his example. They used emails, Excel and notepads — none of them could tell you how many quotes they received a day, nor how many were won, nor what kinds of customers they were.

So when I introduced Julia and Simon to the idea of a CRM system, they were eager to implement it. So eager, in fact, they chose one overnight and mandated that all team members begin using it the very next day.

When the phone rang or an enquiry came through via email, the team would log into the CRM and enter the customer information, their enquiry and a copy of their quote. For a few days after introducing the CRM, Simon would log in, see the information appearing and delight in the success of the project. Problem solved.

A few weeks later, however, Julia walked past an estimator's desk and saw a full note pad of enquiries — phone numbers, product part numbers, notes — none of which had been entered into the CRM.

A few weeks after that Simon received a call from a customer saying she had been waiting four days for a response to her email. He checked the CRM system, and her enquiry wasn't in there. When he raised it with the team, they all looked at each other sheepishly. 'It's taking us three times longer than usual to use the CRM system', one of the members said. 'It's a waste of time!'

Another admitted, 'We're already emailing them and quoting them and doing all the numbers. It's taking us so much longer to input the information twice.'

Simon asked, 'So who is looking after the enquiry from Tabitha? She called me yesterday asking why she hadn't received a response.'

When nobody knew, it suddenly became quite obvious to Simon that collecting knowledge was only part of the issue. Enquiries were slipping through the cracks and Leads they had spent lots of money acquiring (not to mention Customers he had spent years building relationships with) were likely never coming back.

If you've tried to use a CRM system before, these concerns may seem all too real. I've met hundreds of business owners frustrated by the ineffectiveness of their CRM system, thinking that the technology is the reason for the continued lack of growth.

I've also met hundreds of businesses who thrive with an effective CRM, and I've come to recognise the key differences between the two organisations, especially in the way they introduced it into their company.

INTRODUCING IT SLOWLY

Any time I see any technology being thrown into a small business, or any business landscape, I'm always nervous about the outcome, because technology is never the solution: the solution is always the change that happens as a result. For example, everything that Simon wants to achieve with a CRM can be done through any kind of information-collection discipline — recording it in an Excel spreadsheet, on a centralised whiteboard or even a communal notebook. The change required to break existing habits of just reactively responding to enquiries instead of recording them and methodically responding is a lot bigger than the technology itself. Any change management expert will tell you that unless you can break and reform organisational habits, there is no way any kind of new process will stick. And the organisations that tackle this slowly and methodically will always end up with something that sticks rather than something that is haphazardly used.

OBSESSING OVER IT

Simon checked the CRM a few days after implementing it, concluding it was on track, only to find out it very much wasn't on track. The organisations I've seen that have the greatest amount of success with CRM systems are ones that completely integrate the technology into their way of work. It becomes their arm. A second brain. It is the first thing they open in the morning. It is pored over and discussed and debated until everyone is completely comfortable with it.

Simon's second attempt at CRM implementation mirrored a lot of these behaviours. He spent days with the team, practicing inputting enquiries, telling stories and sharing information about customers. They took time to give and get feedback from each other on how to use it better. He had all quotes feed automatically into the CRM so that was where Leads arrived, which took the team off their emails and out of their notebooks. It was becoming part of how the team performed their role.

MAKING IT THE PLACE OF TRUTH

Companies that use a CRM for all their data, use it as their place of absolute truth. If it's not in the CRM system, it didn't happen. So when the team is held accountable to KPIs or the company reflects on results, all the numbers come directly out of the CRM. Because of this, these numbers have to be correct.

Simon's team, although taking longer at first, was back to its usual response time within a month and was building efficiencies every day.

Eventually, Simon's team doubled its conversion rate just through effective recording and compilation of information in the CRM system. And after implementing the next five fundamentals, the team was converting at well over 50 per cent within a year.

2. Add value for free

A simple yet powerful tool in your sales and marketing repertoire is non-monetary value that you add to your products and services. If you recount the story I told about the barber shop in chapter 2, you'll remember that the act of turning on the TV for the man getting his hair cut added perceived value to the product that made the man choose it (or subsequently not choose it again when it was removed).

The same principle needs to be applied to your sales system in order to increase your conversions and create Customers and Fans. As a sole trader or owner, you would have naturally added value to all your interactions with Leads. As a response to that value, the Customer would have been more motivated to buy from you over others. The reason is as simple as this: reciprocity.

The rule for reciprocity is simple: we should repay in kind what another person has provided for us. As humans, we often feel we have an obligation to give and an obligation to repay. This rule works not only with people you know, but also with strangers. It's a human characteristic that often means that value donated rather than paid for is often repaid, in this instance, by choosing to purchase your products over another's.

Here's an example.

Tabitha, a client of Simon's, originally reached out on her quest for product bearings, to three different companies.

Company 1 sent through a quote to Tabatha for the bearings she specified. A few days later they followed up with a call.

Company 2 sent through a quote to Tabatha for the bearings she specified, and also an alternative brand for her consideration. A few days later they followed up with a call.

Simon, however, called Tabitha right away. He got to know her situation, her project and exactly which of his products would meet the requirements of her project. He understood that she was also looking for a fast turnaround; therefore, when he sent through a quote, he included the bearings she requested, but also a quote for a set of bearings that were identical in specs, but could arrive that week. He also let her know he had called the supplier to check that they were in stock and confirmed the delivery schedule.

Tabitha called him to confirm right away and placed the order.

Although nothing monetary was given, Simon added value to the interaction in such a way that Tabitha's refusal would have broken her natural instinct to reciprocate.

When Simon handed over his sales role to his estimating team, all their interactions mimicked Company 1 in the scenario. His team wasn't displaying non-conformance — they were doing what was asked of them — but Simon's way of selling was adding so much value that it was proving impossible for someone to say no.

3. Don't be a hero

If you've made your way through chapter 4, you may have come across my warning about positioning yourself as the hero of the story instead of the customer.

What this means in a sales context is, the more you talk about yourself, the more disconnected you become from the customer. Nobody wants to be in a conversation where they feel ignored. In fact, most people relish the opportunity to talk about themselves, and they feel *more* connected to their subject the less their subject speaks.

When trying to turn a Lead into a Customer, your ability to focus on them in any conversation — their problems, their situation, their desires — is going to determine how successful the outcome will be.

And when you take the time to understand someone's internal problems, you'll be rewarded with connection and also a greater probability of your products being chosen over others'.

In the previous example, Simon called Tabitha back in response to her quote and took the time to get to know her. He asked only leading questions (e.g. no questions that ended with one-word answers), and he maintained a curiosity with her answers. He practiced empathy with her situation, and tried to search for internal problems he could remedy with his products and services. Some questions you might consider to practice this in your organisation are:

- What are your current challenges?
- How do you see our product fitting into your business strategy?
- What specific benefits are you hoping for?
- What other options have you considered?

- How do you see our product helping you achieve your goals?
- Tell me about your decision-making process for purchasing products like this.

Pair these questions with overall conversation tips, such as:

- starting with a friendly introduction
- listening actively and demonstrating genuine interest
- offering on-the spot value
- ending the conversation with a promise to deliver something, then delivering it (e.g., I will send you a quote in an hour).

4. Follow up all leads

After you send through a quote or message to a Lead, it is absolutely essential that you have a mechanism to follow them up. You need a rule or a method of contacting that potential Customer at a certain time *after* you have asked them to purchase.

Often in business we are scared of the follow-up because we don't want to seem pushy or disruptive; however, not following up is significantly more damaging. Why?

- Customers simply forget. Our attention spans as humans are very short and it is easy to completely forget we even asked for a quote.
- Competitors will follow up and win the sale instead.
- Your credibility will be damaged. Leads may perceive you as being unprofessional or unreliable in comparison to a business that does follow up.
- Contact always increases the need for reciprocation. If you've gone out of your way to call, a customer is more likely to respond.

It is essential that you decide (as a group) on what a reasonable follow-up process is. As I experienced personally with Amanda and her skirting boards, I got a string of sporadic follow-up emails. This inconsistency and inattention to detail made me feel less valued than if I received no follow up at all. So before considering how you are going to follow up, it is important to agree on and commit to how often you can follow up reasonably.

A sample of this is:

- quote delivery

- three days later: follow-up phone call

- two weeks later: follow-up email (you might want to add some free value in this email)

- one month later: final follow up email.

A CRM system can help you automate some of these tasks, or send reminders to your team so that they never get missed.

Tip: If you are looking for a more gentle, less intrusive way of following up leads, connect with the Lead on social media. Social media is a great connection tool where you can demonstrate more about your company through passive posting.

5. Set and communicate clear goals

A crazy distinguishing factor between companies I have interacted with that are super successful in converting leads to sales and ones that have labelled it as their bottleneck, is the existence of a clear goal. Whether that is a conversion rate goal, a number of customers goal or a products-per-order goal, the existence of a number that the team or the company is pushing for each month creates momentum that will almost always generate the change required to reach it.

Dale Carnegie's book *How to Win Friends and Influence People* illustrates the powerful influence that numbers and the gamification of those numbers can have on individuals and teams. In his story,

Dale talks about the Bethlehem Steel Company who (accidentally) introduced a gamification technique to increase production output. They began displaying the production output of the day shift and night shift so that the alternate team would arrive at the factory wanting to beat or improve upon the other team's number.

Such a technique turned the simple act of delivering on KPIs into a game that spurred on individuals and teams to reach it.

In companies where there are marketing and sales silos, having clearly defined, collaborative and communicated numbers brings them together. In large teams, repeating goals as the purpose of their day's work makes it everybody's business and encourages collaboration and teamwork. And using a CRM system ensures these numbers are easy to manage and access — without them, it is near-impossible to know how you are going across your entire customer journey.

6. Create consistency

Lastly, and most importantly, is consistent delivery. As with the entire customer journey system and The Very Good Marketing Model, consistency is what enables you to maintain better-than-benchmark conversion rates and ensure you are setting your business up for long-term success.

What Simon discovered when he began overhauling the sales and estimating team, was that every person within the group communicated with Leads differently. Some would build rapport over the phone before emailing through a quote, some would email back a quote straight away. Some would happily chat to Leads in the mornings, but in the afternoons would be short and blunt over the phone. One of his team members flat out refused to attach any brochures or collateral to emails.

Instead of presenting as a strong, single entity, Simon's business was as successful as the mood of the person who answered the phone.

To remedy this, Simon needed to design the sales process that he wanted his team to follow, and ensure that it was followed every time. Only then can he truly know where his business is sitting in terms of its conversion rate, and only then can he work on introducing techniques (such as the ones discussed in this chapter) into the repertoire of his team.

Overselling and underselling

Have you noticed that big businesses frequently credit their growth to having a great 'sales strategy'? What on earth is that, and how can I get my hands on it? Whenever I have asked those leaders exactly what that means, I've never received an answer describing what that strategy is. Eventually, I realised that what those leaders meant was that they had a good salesperson or sales team, not a good sales strategy.

As a growing business, employing a good salesperson may seem like a good thing at the time of recruitment, but often what happens is, as you grow, diversify, change team members or cross geographic locations, it becomes obvious that there is a difference between having a salesperson and having a company sales strategy.

If you are utilising people to convert your Leads to Customers and you're struggling to reach your goals, it could be because one of two things are happening: the first is that your salesperson is overselling and the second is that they are underselling, and both need to be replaced with a company-wide sales strategy.

Overselling

Your organisation may be overselling, and what I mean by this is that you have sales professionals you have hired specifically to undertake selling tasks. They may have been in sales in the past, possibly for a similar industry, and they use their personal experience to do whatever is needed to achieve the sale and earn their keep. Often, the individuals in these roles have bold and energetic personalities — they are 'people people', so they have built numerous personal relationships among customers and stakeholders. They promise customers the world and employ sales techniques by the book to achieve as many conversions as they can. Sometimes they are paid on commission, so they will never work as a team, share their learnings or stick around your organisation for long, which will leave you in a lurch when they resign, you expand or you franchise locations.

Underselling

The reverse of this is underselling. For many organisations, the sales function comprises a group of individuals who receive enquiries and use little to no sales and marketing techniques to perform their role. Instead, they undertake a quoting or estimating procedure to deliver a price to a customer based on the customer's enquiry. Once they send off the estimate, their job is done.

It is usually easy for me to spot the organisations doing this. They are the ones who are generally late to respond to enquiries. Their KPIs are measured by the number of quotes they get out that day or the wait time for a response to a quote, and they usually do not have a method for measuring or tracking their success.

Without any persuasion principles in place or a deliberate strategy for conversion, those customers are either going to choose to do business with other companies that do have those strategies in place or fall back on price to make their choice. Neither of these options is ideal.

Luckily, the antidote for both these scenarios is the same. Creating a company-wide sales process that everyone needs to follow consistently will take the best from the oversellers and provide it to the undersellers to enable everyone to meet in the middle and deliver a good, consistent experience to every Lead.

Creating and delivering a sales process

To begin the process of capturing a sales process, it is important to identify where you have had success in the past. For Simon, it was straightforward: he could go back through five years of successful Lead-to-Customer conversions and pinpoint the most successful conversations, materials, timings and techniques to begin the brainstorm.

This is also a great place for you to start.

Exercise: Sales Process

Time required: 2 hours

Stakeholders: Leadership team, sales or estimating team

Equipment: Whiteboard, pen, paper

Method

1. On a whiteboard, brainstorm all the things that have 'worked' for your salespeople when trying to convert a Lead to a Customer in the past. These can be techniques, steps, marketing materials or messages.

2. Discuss which ones have worked the most frequently and identify any patterns by circling them on the board. These will begin to formulate a detailed sales process for your entire team.

3. Identify your average time to successfully convert a Lead to a Customer (e.g. a day, a week, a month, six months). An easy way to find this is to take your last month's worth of sales and pinpoint when they first contacted you and find the average from that data.

4. Create a sales process timeline from the time Lead is received to the sale, and identify the relevant checkpoints and techniques along that journey that you recognise worked well in the past to develop your sales process.

5. Use this timeline to formalise a high-level sales process that your entire team agrees on.

6. Identify how the sales process fits into a CRM system, what recognisable stages a Lead is at on their way to becoming a Customer and what parts can be automated in a CRM system.

LEAD

KEY ACTIVITY

KEY ACTIVITY

KEY ACTIVITY

CUSTOMER

The process that Simon and his team identified was this:

1. Enquiry received automatically in CRM system.

2. Lead is called via phone within six hours of the enquiry being received. Leading questions are asked to refine the quote and come up with best solution.

3. Quote is sent through immediately after phone call. Two options are always presented.

4. The sales representative or Simon connects with the Lead on LinkedIn.

5. If no response is received after three days, the sales representative calls the Lead. Value is added via phone.(e.g. Simon has negotiated shorter lead times from his supplier so the Lead can have their products sooner).

6. If no response has been received after one week, the Lead is emailed.

7. If no response has been received after two more weeks, the Lead is sent automatic email.

Simon's sales process was fairly simple, but it gave him and his team a starting point that could be amended over time to improve their conversion rate. Unless everyone is delivering the same process, the same way every single time, no improvements are going to stick. You can't improve something that does not exist.

After implementing the 6 fundamentals, Simon's team went from a 10 per cent conversion rate to a near 45 per cent conversion rate in six months — and they are getting better every year. That is over four times the amount of business they were generating just by adapting the way they converted their Leads and creating consistency in their actions. They didn't invest any money into advertising or website development or external contractors; instead they dedicated their time to creating the change they knew would make a real impact on their business for years to come.

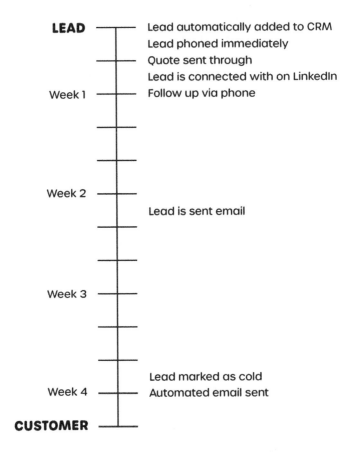

LEAD — Lead automatically added to CRM
Lead phoned immediately
Quote sent through
Lead is connected with on LinkedIn

Week 1 — Follow up via phone

Week 2 —

Lead is sent email

Week 3 —

Lead marked as cold

Week 4 — Automated email sent

CUSTOMER —

The simplicity of repairing this bottleneck in your business is that, if your business is small and agile, change can happen almost instantly. And then you can spend time taking the conversion rates to levels beyond what has been achieved by introducing consistency — perhaps by implementing leading sales techniques from sales strategists around the globe. The opportunities are endless.

In a nutshell

In this chapter, we brought the sales process into a marketing context, and discussed how viewing this as part of your marketing system is essential to business growth. We reviewed the 6 fundamentals of converting Leads to Customers:

1. Effective use of a customer relationship management (CRM) system

CRM systems are an essential ingredient in supporting the Lead-to-Customer process. They automate tasks, enable consistency and ensure everyone is on the same page when it comes to customer interactions and data.

2. Add value for free

A simple yet powerful tool in your sales and marketing repertoire is non-monetary value that you can add to your products and services to engage the human instinct of reciprocity.

3. Don't be a hero

Focus as much as you can on your potential customers in any sales conversation: their problems, their situation, their desires. This is a significant contributor to the conversion rate of this part of your customer journey.

4. Follow up all leads

After you send through a quote or message to a Lead, it is absolutely essential that you have a mechanism for following them up; that is, a rule or a method of contacting that potential Customer at a certain time after you have asked them to purchase.

5. Set and communicate clear goals

Setting a goal that the sales team or the company is pushing for each month creates momentum that will almost always generate the change required to reach it. CRM systems make it easy to determine how close you are to these goals, and they often unify siloed teams.

6. Create consistency

Consistency is what enables you to maintain better-than-benchmark conversion rates and ensure you are setting your business up for long-term success. Eliminate overselling and underselling by designing a sales process that everyone in the organisation can follow and improve on over time.

☐   Exercise to complete: Sales Process

SEVEN

HOW TO TURN A CUSTOMER INTO A FAN

Ah, Fans (sigh). What a desirable status for your customers on their journey. Incredibly loyal, totally profitable and infinitely valuable, your Fans are the key to creating a business that resembles your biggest goals. This part of your customer journey, and the marketing work you perform across this stage and the next, are the beginnings of your change in approach toward marketing forever.

As you know, I am a big believer in the impact that focusing on your Fans will have on your business. This is backed up by a notable principle circulating the business world: the 70/30 rule.

The 70/30 rule is a principle that states that a business should focus on retaining and growing its existing customer base, rather than constantly seeking out new Customers. According to the rule, a business should aim to spend 70 per cent of its time and resources on maintaining and growing its current customer base, and only 30 per cent on acquiring new Customers.

There are several reasons why the 70/30 rule is important for businesses, particularly those with a large number of Fans. For one, it's generally easier and more cost-effective to retain and grow an existing customer base than it is to constantly seek out new customers. Your Fans are more likely to make repeat purchases and refer others to the business, which can help drive long-term growth.

The exact origins of the 70/30 rule are unclear, and it's possible that the concept has been around for some time in various forms. However, the 70/30 rule is often attributed to Frederick Reichheld, a business consultant and author of *The Loyalty Effect*, who is known for his work on customer loyalty and the role it plays in business success. The idea of retaining and growing an existing customer base, rather than constantly seeking out new Customers, is even more pertinent for small businesses who have smaller marketing budgets to attract Strangers and less time to spend finding new opportunities.

This chapter begins the realisation of the 70/30 rule by changing the way you look at your product and service delivery to maximise the number of people evolving from Customer status to Fan status. And believe me, it has so much more to do with marketing than most people realise. Any investment here is an investment that will change your business forever.

The growth dilemma

Remember Helen from the start of the book? Helen's property management company manages and maintains residential rental properties on behalf of landlords. Her customers (the landlords) rely on her for financial management and rent collection, inspections, maintenance requirements, finding tenants and ensuring the smooth running of their commercial assets.

When Helen started her business, she was the one-stop shop for her customers. She was available 24/7 for her landlords and their tenants. She visited properties regularly, she responded quickly to enquiries, and she ensured tenants paid her clients on time, every time. It was the reason her business grew so quickly.

Now with eight staff members, 309 properties to manage and two kids of her own, it was near impossible to maintain the same product delivery standards her most loyal Fans were accustomed to. In fact, not only was she neglecting to turn Customers into Fans like she used to, but she was also actually losing more Customers than she was bringing in.

When I first met Helen, she told me she needed more Customers in the door, which required more Strangers to be attracted. She was not growing (as she had hoped she would continue to do year on year), and was instead shrinking at an alarming rate.

'Where are they going?' I asked Helen over coffee.

'To competitors with cheaper prices, who are promising them the world', Helen said. 'I know my service is better; they are just getting tricked by good salespeople.'

While Helen was certain her product delivery was perfect and it was beyond her control whether someone stayed or left, I had a suspicion that may not have been the reality. And I knew what needed to be done to know for sure.

Net promoter score

A sure-fire way to identify how many of your customers are turning into Fans is to harness the net promoter score (NPS) survey.

NPS is a way for a businesses to measure how likely their Customers are to repurchase, refer or review (aka become a Fan). It's based on a single question that asks Customers to rate their likelihood of recommending the business on a scale from 0 to 10.

Customers who give a high score, like a 9 or 10, are called 'promoters', and are considered loyal and satisfied. Customers who give a lower score, like a 7 or 8, are called 'passives', and may not be as loyal. Customers who give a score of 0 to 6 are called 'detractors', and are considered unhappy with the business.

Many businesses all over the world use this survey to track their customers' happiness, so it is a great tool for benchmarking yourself against other businesses, and a great tool for Helen to identify whether her customers are happy with her service.

From Helen's 309 properties, she could identify 119 unique landlords, and each of them received an email the following week with the question: 'On a scale of 0 to 10, how likely are you to recommend our company to a friend or colleague?' She also included an open-ended question box for comments.

The results for Helen's survey were as follows:

+ 9–10 (promoters): 16 (16 per cent of answered)

+ 7–8 (passives): 45 (45 per cent of answered)

+ 0–6 (detractors): 38 (38 per cent of answered)

+ Unanswered: 20.

Helen had over twice as many detractors as she had promoters, and only 16 per cent of her Customers were going on to become Fans. It was not the news she was hoping for.

Helen's business is different to many others, in the sense that she is constantly delivering a service to customers (versus a company that sells products, for example), and her business heavily relies on the subscription of her customers to generate revenue. Therefore, any weaknesses in the way she delivers her products can have a big impact on the success of her entire business.

In fact, her average yearly management fee sits at around $3000 per property, and she manages 2.5 properties per customer. She also estimates each Fan would remain a Fan for at least six years, based on average ownership rates and her prior experience. Therefore, losing one Fan costs her business approximately $45 000 over a six-year period.

Helen needed to turn her product delivery around — and quickly — to ensure that her business had more promoters than detractors, and that those promoters, or Fans as I prefer to call them, continue to remain with her business for years to come.

Exercise: Identify your NPS

Time required: 4 hours

Stakeholders: Marketing professionals or technical support

Equipment: Survey tool

Method

1. Select a survey software tool (e.g. Survey Monkey) that can support your company to collect NPS feedback from your customers at key intervals:

   - ☐ For annuity businesses (like Helen's), survey customers every three to six months

   - ☐ For other businesses (like Simon's), survey customers four weeks after each purchase, but not twice within a six-month period

2. Automate the survey to send to Customers at set intervals, and collect the data over time to track trends and changes.

3. Collect any additional anecdotal feedback from open-ended question boxes, and review on a regular basis.

Identifying your NPS is going to help you monitor the conversion rate between Customers and Fans in your customer journey. This conversion rate (measured as the percentage of promoters) is a figure that should improve as you work through the remainder of this chapter, and over time. Your goal is to eventually spend 70 per cent of your time finessing this conversion, as well as turning Fans into Jam (as we will work on in the next chapter).

However, resist the urge to start making changes right away. If you've read chapter 6, you may remember how real change takes time, and Simon discovered the hard way that old habits are hard to break. Start with consistency instead, and then level up, which is exactly what Helen set out to do.

Setting the bar

Much like Simon was experiencing within his estimating team, Helen discovered that most of the phone calls and interactions with clients and tenants were all over the place. When an angry tenant phoned one of her team members, that team member changed their tone for every subsequent caller for the rest of the day, sometimes even multiple days.

When the weather was poor, and team members were fielding weather-related phone calls and emails constantly, Helen noticed the response time and quality of responses getting worse and worse. She also noticed the dramatic uplift in general conversations on a Friday, with staff taking more time to chat and display empathy than any other day of the week.

In chapter 2, when we discussed the story of the man visiting the barbershop, the same thing was happening. The man in the story visited three times, and each time his experience got worse and worse.

It wasn't due to a poor-quality product, but his service experience was inconsistent, and he felt like he was getting short changed.

So, before the bar is raised (in terms of maximising the number of Customers we can turn into Fans), it is essential that all your staff can deliver service levels at a clearly articulated bar — and that the service level never drops.

Defining the bar

Similar to creating a sales process, identifying the process to deliver your products is also an essential part of growing your organisation. Perhaps you want to expand production overseas, franchise your business or double the size of your team. In these instances, it is essential that you achieve consistency. There are many examples of businesses that have achieved success by consistently delivering their products or services to their customers. McDonalds and Starbucks are the pinnacle of building loyal customers through consistency. Not glamour or quality of product: consistency.

So where can you set the bar today to ensure it is delivered at this level (not higher, not lower) for an extended period of time?

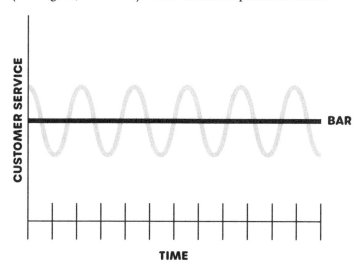

Helen sat down to do just that. Forgetting what she used to deliver as a sole trader, she evaluated her product delivery process from the following angles, and looked at what:

+ was currently being delivered

+ her customers were saying (feedback from her NPS)

+ her competitors were doing.

She then created a list of five non-negotiables (two customer service and three behind-the-scenes business processes) that formed her product delivery:

1. Maximum response time (12 hours for clients, 36 hours for tenants)

2. Open-ended phone calls (30 seconds minimum on seeking to understand, building relationships or adding value at the start of a call)

3. Backup support (additional staff always available during busy periods or to cover leave)

4. Self-service answers available to tenants (a list of the most frequently asked questions by tenants made available on her website)

5. Customer service escalation (all negative disputes are immediately escalated to the leadership team).

Helen knew that, for most of the year, her team could hit that maximum response rate. She also knew that they aimed to build rapport with clients on every phone call. But by creating the business disciplines that could support that, she was more confident that her team could hit that bar 100 per cent of the year. And, over time, they did. Seven months later, she surveyed her customers again, and the results for Helen's second survey were as follows:

- 9–10 (promoters): 24 (25 per cent of answered)

- 7–8 (passives): 55 (56 per cent of answered)

- 0–6 (detractors): 18 (18 per cent of answered)

- Unanswered: 22.

Helen had increased her conversion rate (from Customers to Fans) by at least 50 per cent just by creating a consistent experience for her customers. What do you have to do to ensure you can guarantee a consistent experience for your Customers all year round? What kind of business processes do you have to look at? What kind of customer service initiatives can be automated?

Only once you have achieved consistency (and for Helen this took seven months), can you then begin to raise the bar.

Raising the bar

The good news at this stage is that raising the bar is significantly easier than hitting the bar when it comes to product delivery. Achieving consistency is the hardest bit. But once you have something that exists, it is a lot easier to add on something else and do it consistently, because you already have the mechanisms in place for creating and sticking with the change.

So once Helen had her team delivering at the bar she had set, it was easy for her to have the team implement something new as part of the existing process. For example, Helen knew how important property visits were to her customers, and with the growing business, it was harder for her team to find the time. So when she introduced personal property inspections as a six-monthly initiative, it was something her team took seriously and did not miss. Interestingly, this initiative, which turned out to be something her team enjoyed doing, was one of the biggest game changers for her company because it improved the relationship between her company and her clients, between her clients and the tenants and, subsequently, between the tenants and her company. It gave her team the opportunity to be proactive rather than reactive, and as long as she could continue to deliver this as part of her offering, she could almost guarantee her business would continue to thrive.

The way that Helen raised the bar is what we call 'surprise and delight'. It is one of three key bar-raising techniques that a) don't cost a significant amount, b) aren't hard to implement and c) generate a load of Fans.

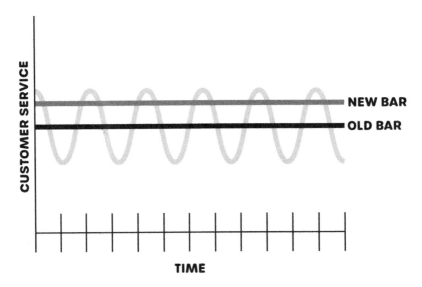

Surprise and delight

Imagine walking into a barber to get your hair cut and being offered a beer. You weren't expecting it, it isn't anything extravagant, but it's a nice surprise. It leaves you feeling delighted at the additional value you didn't pay for, but you received anyway.

This is a great example of the product delivery technique 'surprise and delight'. It is a way of adding value to your product when customers least expect it, converting them to a Fan and beginning the process of generating referrals and reviews for your business.

Surprising your Customer with value when they least expect it does not have to be something that costs money or anything extravagant. It could simply be a follow-up call to see how their recent product or service is going. It could be an email on their birthday, or a handwritten note inside their shipping package.

A client of ours made and sold beautiful handmade rugs. The rugs were custom designed for the client, and were handmade overseas in a small, local community in Sri Lanka, using materials from local farms. The waiting time for these rugs from order to delivery was approximately 12 weeks. Since it was such a long product delivery process, our client set up a few additional touchpoints after they placed the order, but before the product arrived, that went above and beyond customer expectations.

The first touchpoint was two weeks after the customer's order had been placed. It was an emailed photograph of their rug beginning to be manufactured, and the team of people who would be working on it. The second was a handwritten note that thanked the customer for supporting the local manufacturing community, with information about funds that were being donated on their behalf to a local project.

While they are only small things, both were embedded in the product delivery process to highlight the fact that, whilst almost all Australian furniture and homewares are manufactured overseas, this company took great care and effort to support and highlight the individuals who contributed to the manufacturing process. It is a surprise that is guaranteed to create Fans, and it was virtually no effort at all.

When considering what kind of surprise and delight you can use to raise your product delivery bar and turn more Customers into Fans, have a think about what your customers want beyond what you are about to deliver to them. What intrinsic needs do they have? What would make their experience with you that tiny bit better?

Remember that humans possess many intrinsic desires that include, but are not limited to, conserving resources, gaining resources, contributing to something bigger than themselves, gaining social status, being connected and feeling secure. In the rug example, our client harnessed the client's desire to be part of something bigger than themselves (they were doing 'good' for a local community) as well as perhaps building social status with a beautiful rug.

In Helen's example, her site visits spoke to the gaining resources side of her customers. They felt like they got a bonus service for their money, which, in turn, improved the relationship with their tenants that would lead to an undisputed rent rise and even a longer-term tenancy.

Exercise: Surprise and Delight

Time required: 2 hours

Stakeholders: Leadership team, marketing professional, product developer

Equipment: Whiteboard

Method

1. Brainstorm ways that you can add value outside of your current product offering by answering the question: What do my customers really want? What would delight them? What are they not expecting?

2. From that list, choose one item that has a good balance between big impact and little investment. Remember to start small! And then build it into your product delivery process so it naturally becomes part of the way you deliver your products and services.

3. Re-measure your NPS after six months to see if it has improved the outcome.

4. Repeat the process over time if you have other ideas you want to try.

Marginal gains

Once your product delivery bar is set, you are essentially committing to a consistently average product or service for an extended period, when perhaps you were aiming for something a bit higher. Helen, who had always exceeded the product delivery provided by her competitors, was reluctant to scale back her expectations of her product delivery to guarantee consistency, but understood how important it was to build back her Fan base.

But does that mean your product delivery bar always needs to be set at average to ensure consistency? How can you begin the slow and steady process of making improvements to the critical and the non-essential elements that make up your product delivery. Rather than re-imagining your entire product delivery process, you can enact small changes that stick, for example, the:

◆   way your receptionist answers the phone

◆   way your products are packaged before they are shipped out

◆   way your customer receives an invoice

◆   finishing touches on your products.

Separately, these are all very small parts of the way you deliver your products and services; however, a slight improvement in each of them can create a significant impact on your business and the experience of your customers.

Improve a hundred things by just 1 per cent, and you will have a significant competitive advantage over your competitors, and a product delivery process that increases the likelihood your one-time customers will become lifetime customers.

A famous example of marginal gains affecting performance is from the British Cycling organisation, which began the process of harnessing marginal gains back in 2003 to transform the performance of their athletes for the Olympic Games. British Cycling's performance director, Dave Brailsford, pioneered the strategy with great success. 'The whole principle', Brailsford explained to the BBC, 'came from the idea that if you broke down everything you could think of that goes into riding a bike, and improve it by 1 percent, you will get a significant increase when you put them all together.'

Just five years after Brailsford began this process, the British Cycling team dominated the road and track cycling events at the 2008 Olympic Games in Beijing, where they won 60 per cent of the gold medals available, having never excelled in these events before.

Too often, we convince ourselves that massive success requires massive redevelopment or innovation. Just 1 per cent is all you need. When you are evaluating your product delivery process, look for simple ways that you can improve a handful of things by 1 per cent. Sometimes these things might be obvious, sometimes you will have to try hard to go above and beyond. Think of the things your competitors aren't doing but you wish you could receive as a Customer.

Then implement them, one at a time, bit by bit, until they become your new bar, and repeat the process regularly — perhaps forever. Over time, your product delivery will be completely different, and for the better.

As part of this process, Simon and Julia implemented a 'straight' initiative, which saw everyone in their packing warehouse focus their attention on packaging outgoing parts with straight packing tape at perfect right angles. This may seem like a small change, but it contributed to a larger movement of care and attention to packing products that was noticed by their customers.

Exercise: Marginal Gains

Time required: 1 hour

Stakeholders: Leadership team, product delivery team

Equipment: Whiteboard

Method

1. Brainstorm ways of improving any stage of the product delivery process by 1 per cent.

2. Write down all the ideas on a whiteboard, encouraging team members to add to it over the course of a month.

3. At the end of the month, choose one to five ideas (depending on the size and scope of your organisation) and implement the changes, monitoring the consistency of the delivery and permanency of the adjustment.

4. After the change has become permanent, repeat the exercise, choosing another handful of ideas. Repeat forever.

5. Re-measure your NPS after six months to see if it has improved the outcome.

Customer service excellence

Nothing spoils a good product more than bad customer service before, during or after the sale. I can give you a list of all my favourite places that I would frequent until a bad run of customer experience turned me away forever, despite the product quality. My motto is: 'Disappoint me once, shame on you. Disappoint me twice, shame on me.'

If your products and services are delivered by humans, there is every chance that the customer service levels are not delivered consistently. Such was the case for Helen's team, but it is also the case for every business, physical product or not.

Whilst setting the bar in terms of consistently delivering your products and services is important, setting a good customer service bar is equally — if not more — important. It's often the case that the idea of 'good customer service' varies not only across businesses but between individuals within those businesses. Similarly, what you may think is terrible customer service may be perceived as good customer service by the person delivering it.

An example of this is trying to order a coffee from a cashier who spends the whole conversation with you watching a group of customers behind you, who doesn't look you in the eye once, repeatedly asks you to repeat what you said, who doesn't smile and simply walks away whilst your transaction is processing.

This person may believe their customer service is perfectly fine, but it is not what you may consider to be 'good customer service', and that will impede your ability to transition from Customer to Fan.

What business owners consider 'good customer service' compared with the people they employ is actually a very common misalignment. This makes agreeing on what constitutes a good customer service bar incredibly important. And ensuring your team members can stick to that in good times, as well as in bad times, is essential.

Remember, it is how you act in times of adversity that really define who you are, not how you act when things are easy. Customers will respect you more if you display empathy during challenges, but that is often the first time that 'good' customer service disappears.

So how can you capture what 'good customer service' looks like for your organisation, and set a bar that can be delivered at a consistent and sustainable level? What does that level even look like?

Exercise: Customer Service

Time required: 4 hours, repeated twice, 4 months apart

Stakeholders: Leadership team, customer service consultant (optional)

Equipment: Whiteboard, pen, paper, computer

Method: Part 1

1. Clearly define your current customer service level. Explain what things are done well and what things can be improved.

2. Brainstorm what 'good customer service' looks like amongst everyone in the room and what standard-level experience you would like every customer to have.

3. Focus on transitioning your current practices into this new reality of 'good customer service', delivered the same every time. This may take time, but set yourself a goal to re-measure your NPS after four months to see if it has improved the outcome.

Method: Part 2: Four months later

1. Using your previous work on what 'good customer service' looks like, brainstorm what 'great customer service' looks like to everyone in the room. Ideally, you will focus on aspirational, but achievable, behaviours your staff can implement.

2. Focus on transitioning your current practices from 'good' to 'great' customer service. What steps can you take to achieve this? What support does your team need to be able to implement these actions?

3. Choose one thing to work on at a time until it is mastered and is a consistent part of your product delivery process. Don't move on until the bar is set and solid.

4. Re-measure your NPS after six months to see if it has improved the outcome.

The mindset needed to create lifetime Fans

As a Visionary (rather than a Technician working in the business) your mindset needs to be laser focused on converting Customers into Fans. The 70/30 rule should be an obsession of yours, to the point where you start comparing your NPS results with industry trailblazers, like Apple or Amazon.

This means working your way towards delivering an exceptional customer experience. Apple's customer experience reputation wasn't built overnight, but through consistency and commitment it has become world-class on one of the biggest scales ever comprehended.

To get the bar high, and create more Fans than you ever thought you could, you will need to adopt the following mindsets:

1. Customer-centricity: A customer-centric mindset is focused on understanding and meeting the needs and preferences of customers, and putting the customer at the centre of everything you do, as discussed in chapter 4.

2. Innovation: Adopting a mindset focused on innovation means being open to new ideas and approaches. It means constantly seeking ways to improve and innovate in order to deliver a better customer experience and product delivery process.

3. Empathy: A empathetic mindset means being able to understand and relate to customers on an emotional level, and being able to anticipate and address their needs and concerns across every interaction.

4. Authenticity: An authentic mindset involves being genuine in your interactions with customers, and being transparent and honest in your business practices.

By adopting these mindsets across your product delivery process, you can begin the steps towards finding Fans inside your business, and then turning those Fans into revenue for your business. We call this 'making jam'.

In a nutshell

In this chapter, we talked about the most valuable conversion rate in your entire marketing system: turning Customers into Fans. Fans are incredibly valuable for your business, and it has been said that great businesses should implement the 70/30 rule retaining and growing their existing customer base. This means aiming to spend 70 per cent of your time and resources on maintaining and growing your current customer base, and only 30 per cent on acquiring new Customers.

We started this chapter by evaluating your net promoter score (NPS), and using your NPS to determine how well you are converting Customers into Fans. We looked at Helen, the owner of a property management company, who had a lot fewer Fans than she realised, and she used her NPS to discover that.

☐   Exercise to complete: Identify your NPS

Setting the bar

Identifying the process behind delivering your products is an essential part of growing your organisation. Setting the bar is about delivering a consistent experience every single time a Customer interacts with your business after their initial purchase. Work hard to ensure you can deliver your products and services at a set 'bar' level. You will be surprised at how much that improves your NPS.

Raising the bar

Once your bar is set, it can be improved. Raising the bar is about implementing three key strategies that transform your product delivery process.

Surprise and delight: Raise your product delivery bar by introducing ancillary value alongside your products and services.

Marginal gains: Spend time improving your product delivery process by 1 per cent across different areas, and over time you will see a huge improvement in the quality of your product.

Customer service excellence: Slowly turn good customer experiences into great customer experiences by lifting the bar across different customer touchpoints on their way to becoming a Fan.

- ☐ Exercises to complete: Surprise and Delight; Marginal Gains; Customer Service

EIGHT

HOW TO TURN A FAN INTO JAM

Every weekday morning, myself and my colleagues walk down to one of the six coffee shops on our office block. The same one, every single day. And we have done so for nearly two years. It is safe to say that we are Fans of this business, and we estimated that each of us spends around $1300 per year with them. (Crazy right?)

But whether consciously or unconsciously, this coffee shop has turned us into some of the most loyal Fans that any coffee shop could hope for. The other day I arrived with a few others and neglected to order a coffee because I had already had one at home. So when they called my name out, I was surprised. The barista told me that she saw me sitting there and thought I may have forgotten to order, so she made me a coffee anyway. 'Why would I go anywhere else?' I thought to myself.

Another time I was there, the staff brought a cake over to us at our table, sliced into five pieces. She said they were trying a new recipe and wanted us to let her know what we thought.

So when the owner of the restaurant came over and asked me whether I would leave her business a review on Google, I just did it on the spot.

No hesitation whatsoever. This review would help other Strangers come to her business and become Fans, just like me.

Turning Customers into Fans is one of the biggest opportunities that any business has. But what you do with those Fans, how you keep them engaged and how you turn them into further business for your business is equally important.

The small business community has a strange mindset when it comes to engaging with past Customers. I've never worked with a company that already had a system in place for this. Most business owners that I meet either don't collect information about past Customers, don't know how to communicate with them or don't see the value. Instead, they spend their marketing time attracting Strangers.

If this is you right now with your business, then you're not alone. Engaging with Customers is hard work and doesn't pay back immediate rewards. But, believe me, over time, it will. We know this thanks to the 70/30 rule and the evidence of its success across the world for small business.

We discussed the 70/30 rule in chapter 7. It is (just in case you need a refresher) a guideline for customer engagement that suggests that businesses should focus on engaging with their current Customers (the 70 per cent of the customer base) rather than trying to constantly acquire new ones (the 30 per cent). This rule pays off because:

- It increases Customer loyalty: By focusing on engaging with and retaining your Fans, you can build stronger, more loyal relationships, which can help to increase customer retention and reduce churn.

- It increases Customer lifetime value: By retaining your Fans for longer periods of time, you can increase their lifetime value to your business. (Think one $5 coffee vs my $1300 yearly spend.)

- Reduced marketing and acquisition costs: By focusing on engaging with your Fans rather than constantly trying to acquire new ones, you will reduce the marketing cost associated with acquiring Strangers.

So, once you've put the work in to converting Customers into Fans through the way you deliver your products and services, you need to dedicate time to continue engaging those Fans and encourage them to repurchase, refer and leave reviews.

The mindset you need to engage raving Fans

To really transform your business, you need to shift your mindset away from attracting Strangers and towards creating and engaging raving Fans (at least 70 per cent of the time), and it is a big shift. The key elements to this mindset are:

- Believing in the 70/30 rule. Believe it even when you can't understand or see it yet.

- Appreciating the difference between a Customer and a Fan. Calculate the lifetime value of a Fan and remember the difference.

- Treating every single Fan like gold. Treat them the same way you would treat a Lead. Love them. Nurture them. Value them. Connect with them.

- Selling to them. Having them but not engaging with them won't help you reach your goals.

To navigate your way through these mindset changes, I want to tell you the next part of the story about Shane, the coffee roaster. Shane, as I mentioned at the very start of this book, desperately wanted a coffee roasting business. He bought a coffee roaster, found the best suppliers in the world, created an e-commerce website and a brand and then ... nothing. No growth in customers, no new website visitors — in fact, he began losing his contracts with cafés.

Shane was so busy trying to grow by attracting Strangers that he lost the only business that was keeping him afloat: the business generated by his Fans. When cafés began cancelling their contracts, Shane was shocked. He hadn't spoken to any of them in months and assumed everything was going fine.

He started to re-think his entire strategy for his business. Was the product wrong? Was his customer service bad? Was his pricing strategy off? Unfortunately, Shane didn't have a chance to ask his Customers before they left, and adapt his offering accordingly. Instead, he was scrambling to start his business again from scratch. He was in deep, and he was very stressed.

So, when I met Shane, we were really starting from square one. Except this time he was going to do it right. Starting with the Fans he still had.

Believing in the 70/30 rule

Shane's belief in the 70/30 rule didn't come until he had experienced the opposite: losing his Fans and it almost costing him his entire business. For you, who may not have experienced Shane's misfortune, finding the motivation to execute the 70/30 rule should come from your own experiences and the success of companies around you.

Just like the coffee shop on our block, you too will have companies that you are committed to purchasing from again and again — possibly across your favourite technology, clothing, groceries, food and beverage providers, or even niche stores that you have a particular interest in, like homewares or children's toys. Think about what makes you come back again and again. Is it consistent service? Is it additional value? Perhaps you have some kind of loyalty offer with them?

Consider for a moment what ancillary things outside of the actual product make you a Fan of the companies you love, and then think about what that may mean for your company. What kind of things could you do to continue engaging your Fans?

Knowing the lifetime value of your Fans

If Shane took the time to understand the value of his coffee shop customers to his business, he may have changed his approach to marketing and focused 70 per cent of his time on that group instead. So, it is very important to ensure you know these same numbers for your own business.

To calculate the lifetime value (LTV) of your customers, you'll need to consider the following factors:

- Average purchase value: Calculate the average amount of money that a Customer spends on each purchase.

- Purchase frequency: Determine how often a Customer makes a purchase.

- Customer lifespan: Estimate the average length of time that a Customer will continue making purchases from your business. (This is a tough one to estimate. If you don't have historical data, e.g. if your business is relatively new, you can guesstimate through online research of your industry.)

To calculate LTV, you'll need to multiply the average purchase value by the purchase frequency, and then multiply that number by the customer lifespan. For example:

LTV = Average purchase value x Purchase frequency
        x Customer lifespan

So, if the average purchase value is $5, the purchase frequency is once per weekday, and the customer lifespan is three years, the LTV would be:

LTV = 5 x 260 x 3 = $3900

This means that the lifetime value of myself and each of my team members at our favourite coffee shop over the lease of our office is at least $3900.

Calculating this for your business might only be an estimate, but it is essential to shift your mindset into focusing on your Fans.

Exercise: Calculate Your Lifetime Customer Value

Time required: 15 minutes

Stakeholders: Leadership team

Equipment: Calculator, pen, paper

Method

1. Separate your unique markets and gather data about their average purchase price, purchase frequency and lifespan. If your business is new and you don't have historical data, you can search online for the lifespan of a customer in your industry.

2. Use the following formula to determine the lifetime value for each of your target markets:

$$LTV = \text{Average purchase value} \times \text{Purchase frequency} \times \text{Customer lifespan.}$$

Don't worry if you don't have the number perfect.

Connecting with your Fans and treating them like gold

Shane recognised that he had two distinct markets, each with their own lifetime value. The first were coffee shops. Coffee shops ordered 25 kg from him each week on average, at a price of $30 per kg, with an estimated lifespan of two years, that valued them at approximately $78 000.

His other market were consumers, who were buying beans directly from his website. With a subscription model, Shane estimated these consumers would consume 1 kg of coffee every three weeks, at $52 per kg across a six-month lifespan. This gave them a lifetime value of $442.

Both of these groups require some kind of personal connection that builds trust and loyalty between them and Shane's business. This connection is essential to sparking repurchases, referrals and reviews that will continue growing the business.

Back when you first started your business, you would have relied on word of mouth as a marketing method more than anything else. The majority of businesses I meet cite this as their mechanism for growth, and whether you realise it or not, it all stemmed from the connection you built and the engagement you sustained with your Fans.

In my example, the coffee shop I frequented did things like remembering my coffee order, or giving me a free coffee or piece of cake. This was their way of connecting with me and engaging me to keep me as a Fan (whether they knew it or not).

As you grow, it becomes harder and harder to sustain that personal connection, as was the case for Shane, Helen and Simon who all had their attention pulled to different areas of the business as it grew.

For Shane's business, it was imperative that he design a process for connecting with and engaging his Fans in a consistent way — and it is imperative for yours too.

WHAT DOES CONNECTION LOOK LIKE FOR YOUR FANS?

For Shane's two distinct groups of Fans, he needed to identify what 'connection' and 'engagement' looked like so he could create a process for ensuring they trusted him, felt valued and remained loyal.

Connection can look like a lot of different things, but the essence is always about value. How can you show your Fans that you value them? How often should you show them? And how can you do this without it relying on you as the owner? Some ideas for value-based connection for a small business are:

- giving away products or services for free
- giving away knowledge
- providing excellent customer service
- personalising your communication
- getting to know them, using their name, remembering facts
- being vulnerable or open about yourself or your business

- providing additional ancillary value alongside products and services

- asking for their feedback or opinion and implementing it.

All these things do not have to rely on a personal connection from the owner. For example, you can train your staff to implement all these things as part of their customer service.

A client of ours who owns a busy restaurant in the Perth CBD has implemented a policy where all staff members get a $50 credit per month to use as they wish on providing additional value to customers. She gave examples where team members brought out two dishes instead of one when overhearing an undecided customer, or upgrading coffees for regulars who said they have a busy day ahead.

Similarly, a plumbing company that we support has an alert set up on their CRM where on the second and subsequent visits to a home (regardless of the time between visits), the plumber will perform the work they were hired for, and then also treat all the toilets in the home with an enzyme deodorizer for free. It costs them very little money and time but is always appreciated. Before they leave, they offer the customer a magnet with the company details on it, which is almost always accepted and displayed on their fridge. It has increased their number of Fans and their referrals dramatically.

Evaluate what your Fans may find valuable, and brainstorm ways that you can deliver it to them. Then it is a case of codifying it as part of your regular business processes.

HELLO, IT'S ME AGAIN

The coffee shop I frequent sees me almost every day. But regular purchases are not always the buying pattern for every business, so it makes it hard to offer continuous value or build relationships.

If the purchase frequency of your customers is more like weeks or months rather than days, it is essential you continue communicating with them between purchases to nurture that connection. My top three recommendations for this are using phone calls, emails and social media, and providing the same value in a more passive way.

You would have experienced this as a consumer, most likely through email. Businesses will send you emails with discounts or offers, possibly value or behind-the-scenes content that reminds you that they exist and nurtures your relationship.

For Shane, he wanted to try and implement emails as a tool for connecting with both his café customers and e-commerce customers. What Shane did was take what he knew was the cornerstone of his rapid growth at the start of his business and replicate it using email. He began crafting emails like this:

Hi [first name], Shane here from Coffee Company.

I hope that May is treating you well so far?

With the weather warming up in Brazil, we've just gotten word that a new crop of my favourite bean from the Minas Gerais region has been harvested. The farmers, Jacob and Lida, tell me it is one of their best crops yet. Drying is finishing up this week and green beans will arrive early next week for me to roast. I can't wait for you to try it, so for every order you place in May, I'm going to include a 250 g bag of whole beans from Jacob and Lida's farm. Please let me know what you think!

Because of this shipment, I'm currently discounting our Pea Berry coffee by 15 per cent to make room. Here's the link if you want to get your hands on it before it runs out. It's a great bean with a unique flavour profile: perfect for black coffee drinkers.

Have a great day and, like always, please reach out if you have any feedback, questions or concerns about our products and my service — or just to say hi!

Thanks, Shane

Although these emails were being received by multiple people, the way Shane structured them made them appear like the recipient was his only client, and demonstrated how much Shane valued their opinion and their business. Over time, more regular emails like this painted a clear picture of his business, his values and his life, and it was easy to continue maintaining relationships without the time requirement of calling or visiting everyone fortnightly, or the coldness of a generic sales email just offering a 15 per cent discount on Pea Berry coffee.

The same idea could be replicated on social media, and Shane also chose to call each one of his commercial customers monthly to continue strengthening those relationships. Now he had the opportunity to overcome any problems and diffuse any potential risk of the customer changing companies before it was too late.

Exercise: Valuing Your Fans

Time required: 2 hours

Stakeholders: Leadership team, customer service team

Equipment: Whiteboard, computer

Method

1. Brainstorm all the ways you can show value to your current Fans. Brainstorm using questions such as: What do our Customers think is valuable outside of products and services? What does our customer feedback tell us that Customers really appreciate? What would

entertain, delight or inspire our current Customers? What have you experienced as a consumer yourself before that made you feel valued?

2. Boil that list down to realistic actions, meaning what can:

    ◆   actually be achieved (remember that change needs to start small)

    ◆   you afford to do?

3. Introduce just one or two of those tasks into your business or product delivery process bit by bit until they become a regular part of the way you do business. Keep in mind the barber shop story from chapter 2: don't attempt to do something if you can't sustain it, because once you add value, you can't take it away without consequences.

Selling to your Fans

Whilst the process of repurchasing, reviewing your business or referring you to others often comes organically for Fans, a gentle push can help to really supercharge your business growth and your entire marketing system.

This is because the 3 Rs (repurchasing, reviewing and referrals) can create an infinite chain of events that compound over time. One customer can refer you to ten people, who each become Fans and refer you to ten other people. One Fan has now generated 110 new Customers, but without the encouragement, they may only have generated one or two Fans off their own back.

The key to selling to (or asking for something from) your Fans is having the confidence that you have given away enough value that they will gladly take action without hesitation.

In chapter 6, I spoke about reciprocity, and the desire for humans to repay in kind what they have received. When you start the process of showing your Fans how much you value them, the task of asking for something in return will be more successful.

At my local coffee shop, I didn't hesitate to leave them a review on Google when they asked because of the value they had provided to me. It would be different if I were asked to leave a review after walking into a coffee shop I rarely frequented.

Similar to selling to Leads, asking for something from Customers should be done in perfect harmony with adding value. It's a case of give and take, and the frequency of the 'give' versus the frequency of the 'take' will be unique to your business and circumstances.

A good rule to start with may be four 'gives' to one 'take'; for example, my local coffee shop may give me four free coffees before asking me for a review. Or Shane might perform four months of communicating via phone and email before asking for a referral from one of his café clients.

'Taking' one of the 3 Rs may seem daunting at first, but it needs to become a part of your regular business practices in order to grow. So how should a small business implement the three Rs?

The 3 Jam Rs

Having Fans is great, but using those Fans to grow your business is essential. From your Fans, you are going to want to create Jam, and we call it Jam because once you get the process right, it creates an infinite amount of growth for your business. All three of these elements are essential for growth.

Repurchases

Repurchases represent the frequency a Fan will purchase. As part of your lifetime value calculation, you would have identified the average frequency of purchases, and therefore the number of times they generate revenue for your business.

You may be achieving this now organically, just through adding value and engaging with your Fans. However, there are ways that you can encourage more repurchases and ensure your Fans are choosing you every time.

One way to do this is through a rewards system. Implementing a formal system that rewards your Customers for their continued selection of your company over others is a great way of selling to Fans. It could be as simple as a coffee stamp or as complex as a points system that is set up with complementary companies (such as is done by credit card companies). Such systems promote the concept of gamification and encourage fans to keep spending in order to win a prize.

Shane implemented this specifically for his e-commerce customers. At-home coffee drinkers go through, on average, 1 kg of coffee every three weeks, so if they weren't buying from his business, they were likely buying from somewhere else. He brainstormed the things that would make a Fan continue to buy coffee from him every few weeks guaranteed, and came up with a subscription model. Fans could choose their coffee, the amount and the grind type, and it would arrive at their doorstep, hassle-free, every three weeks.

To encourage Customers to do this, Shane decided to offer free shipping on every subscription order of 1 kg or more. It meant that the fans considering this would be incentivised to continue to repurchase because shipping is usually one of the biggest barriers to buying a product online. Commercially, he chose to make it 1 kg to ensure he didn't lose any money on the orders, and knowing that a 1 kg bag would remain fresh for a significant amount of time (ideal for the occasional purchaser).

Rewards systems are in abundance, so if you want to implement one for your Fans, ensure you have something that is enticing and valuable. It's interesting to note that 62 per cent of customers don't feel that the brands they are loyal to do enough in return, so ensure you can deliver something that they are going to tell others about.

Reviews

Great reviews can grow your business faster than any other kind of online content. They create trust and confidence, and demonstrate authority to your potential Customers, helping them see you as a skilled and knowledgeable business with a history of success. I've seen cases where a one-star bump in reviews increased sales by over 5 per cent for a service-based business.

The people best able to review your company are your Fans because they are your biggest advocates. This is different to asking any past Customer for a review without identifying (through your NPS) who the biggest promoters or Fans are, which can end up creating a problem. An example of this is if Helen, the property manager, sent a blanket review request out to all her Customers, 38 per cent of whom were actually detractors. She would likely get more negative reviews than positive ones, which would have the opposite effect for her business.

The best way of obtaining an official review from a Fan is to ask for one (simple), but ensure it is in exchange for enough value that it seems like a really simple and easy task for them. Ensure you provide them with a quick way of doing so (e.g. if you are asking them for the review via email, provide the link for a quick response) and thank them when you receive it.

If you would like to seek a review for your website, you can reach out to a Fan directly with enough information that they'll knock it out of the park. There are a few simple steps you can use as a template to do this.

1. Explain to them what the review will be used for and how much you would appreciate it.

2. Provide them with some guidance on how to write the review (e.g. providing them with prompts such as: What was your biggest challenge? How were we able to help? What is life like now? These three question prompts can help form a very well-rounded and inspiring testimonial).

3. Explain to them how they can provide it so that it is easy (e.g. provide them with a direct link).

4. Thank them for leaving the review and show them a lot of appreciation (seriously, go out of your way to thank them).

Reviews are such a big part of building your authority as a business that this process should not be taken lightly and should be a permanent process within your business. If you're looking for inspiration, have a look at how e-commerce websites such as Amazon or travel websites like TripAdvisor ask for, and showcase, reviews after purchasing. It is an automatic part of their process that, as a consumer, you rely on heavily to make your own purchasing decisions.

Referrals

Referrals (also known as 'word of mouth') are the key to growing your business in an infinite way because they spread the word about your products and services without you having to spend any money on attracting Strangers yourself. You may think that waiting for referrals could take a long time, and there is no way of speeding this process up — but you would be wrong.

There is only one thing you can do to guarantee a steady or growing stream of referrals, and that is to ask for them. If you have given enough value away and you have real Fans who love your business, it would genuinely be their pleasure to receive a little push so that they can further support your business.

To be sure, though, you may want to offer some additional value in exchange for that referral, and a great example of this comes from the successful launch of Dropbox. Dropbox is an online, cloud-storage platform that discovered very quickly that attracting Strangers was not working very well for their business. Because their technology was new and a shift in the way people did things, Strangers needed more convincing to jump on board. They needed convincing from a friend.

Dropbox began focusing on their Fans to drive a referrals program that used the loyalty and enthusiasm of current users to bring Strangers on board, and then rewarded them for it. Dropbox's referral program chose to give away value in the form of additional cloud storage. The offer was 500 MB of free Dropbox space for you and a friend when they signed up.

So, each time they referred a friend, both parties received extra storage. It could be repeated 32 times (as per their terms and conditions), which meant that one Fan could deliver 32 new customers to Dropbox in exchange for something they already had in abundance: cloud storage.

To make taking up this offer attractive and easy, Dropbox used a few key marketing tools:

- Understand the internal needs of customers: Dropbox users wanted more space for the same dollar spend. It was the commodity they cared about.

♦ Used solution-based messaging: The wording Dropbox used to promote this was 'Get more space'. This, instead of 'invite your friends', spoke to the desires of the users and showed Dropbox understood their needs.

♦ Required few brain calories: Humans shy away from anything complex, so Dropbox made it easy to refer in any format (messenger apps, email, SMS, social media), and offered to sync contacts from any email account. They also made the onboarding process for new users incredibly simple so there was no hesitation in inviting your friends

The referrals strategy Dropbox used has been widely attributed to not only their growth, but their survival in the first few years, and really proved the success of the 70/30 rule in a real-life scenario. Dropbox essentially said to their Fans, 'If you refer us to a friend, and they become a customer, we will reward you', and this technique is fairly easy to replicate in your business. Some examples amongst our clients are:

♦ Dance school: 10 per cent discount on your semester fee when you refer someone who signs up.

♦ Golf club: Free bucket of golf balls when you bring a friend to the club with you.

♦ Wedding photographer: Free one-year anniversary photography session for a referral who purchases a wedding package.

As for Shane, he chose to introduce a referrals program for his café customers, offering them 20 per cent off their order for three months if they referred another café that signed up with his company. Knowing that most café owners knew other café owners, and the lifetime value of each one was so high, he was confident that the relative cost of the deal was a lot less than the cost of him going out and acquiring Strangers as café customers — and it worked. Shane was able to build up his café customer base again within four months, and even won back some of the clients he lost.

After the success of this referrals campaign, he tried the exact deal (20 per cent off for three months) for his subscription customers on his e-commerce store, and saw a good response too.

Shane continued trying different mixes of offers for his Fans over time, experimenting with his regular Fan emails to identify what deals or offers resonated with the different groups best until he was confident enough to bring an offer like this to his wider customer base.

Exercise: The 3 Jam Rs

Time required: 2 hours

Stakeholders: Leadership team, customer service team

Equipment: Whiteboard, computer

Method

1. Brainstorm ways of increasing your repurchase rate from your current Fans.

2. Brainstorm ways to ask for reviews as part of your current product delivery or business processes.

3. Brainstorm ways to speed up the referrals process for your current Fans, whether that is simply asking for referrals or trading them for something of value.

4. Introduce each of them into your business gradually until they stick and begin delivering value.

5. Review each of them regularly to see what kind of impact they are having and if you have to tweak your approach for maximum impact.

In a nutshell

In this chapter, we focused on how to use your Fans to create Jam or, to put it simply, how to use them to make your business money. We talked about the key mindset shifts you need to engage your raving Fans.

Believing the 70/30 rule

The 70/30 rule is a guideline for customer engagement that suggests that businesses should focus on engaging with their current Customers (the 70 per cent of the customer base), rather than trying to constantly acquire new ones (the 30 per cent). Use your own experience as a consumer to ensure you believe in this rule 100 per cent.

Knowing the lifetime value of your Fans

Calculate and appreciate just how much a Fan is worth to you by using the lifetime value (LTV) formula: LTV = Average purchase value x Purchase frequency x Customer lifespan.

☐ Exercise to complete: Calculate Your Lifetime Customer Value

Connecting with your Fans and treating them like gold

Personally connecting with your customers as you grow is hard. Take the time to recognise the value you are providing to your Fans, and identify how you can continue to do this on a bigger scale. Shane did this by mimicking personalized emails and bringing his Fans into his day-to-day life.

☐ Exercise to complete: Valuing Your Fans

The 3 Jam Rs

Having Fans is great, but using those Fans to grow your business is essential. The 3 Jam Rs are about driving repurchases, reviews and referrals from your current Fan base in a way that is effortless and organic.

☐   Exercise to complete: The 3 Jam Rs

BRINGING IT ALL TOGETHER

What a journey we have been on together. Whether you have read the chapters in order and made it here in one sitting, or you've adventured through this book — beating one bottleneck at a time — reaching the end is always a relief. You made it!

The truth is that the journey from Technician to Visionary is a long one, but a lot of the principles we have learnt here are the same ones that are going to support you to bring a visionary mindset into all areas of your business. These include:

- Systems thinking: the process of creating systems within your business, and working on system inefficiencies, such as bottlenecks

- Goal setting and communication: getting really clear about what success looks like to you and sharing it with others

- Practicing consistency and creating organisation-wide processes: formalising how you do things and doing it the same way every time

- Eliminating biases and cognitive dissonance: recognising where your own thoughts may be limiting your business decisions

- Going slow: permanent change takes time, so make changes slowly but consistently

- Collecting insightful data: contextualising data (such as conversion rates) and collecting it often to give you a true insight into your business.

Throughout this book, we covered a lot of marketing concepts and theories that you may not have come across before that may feel overwhelming. You may also be concerned about committing to a new framework and abandoning any marketing you already have in place. These are reasonable concerns, especially when it comes to your business and the decisions you make. This is why we have spent years rigorously testing the framework and the concepts across a variety of businesses. What we found time and time again was that the simplicity of The Very Good Marketing Framework and the approach to beating bottlenecks was creating an immediate sense of relief for owners (who were trying to 'do it all'), and enabled them to take small steps with confidence, which ultimately led to incredible results.

As you close the pages of this book, I hope it will only be for now and not forever. The key to The Very Good Marketing Framework is applying the five Cs continuously to your marketing, one of them being 'constant improvement'. This requires you to keep revisiting your bottlenecks to improve them as consumer behaviour changes, your business grows and technology evolves.

At any time, you can visit verygoodmarketing.com.au and take a further dive into this framework and applying it to your business. I have assembled worksheets, resources and further content for businesses to harness, depending on the bottleneck you are trying to beat and the industry you are in.

Finally, if growing a small business has taught me anything, it is that all good things take time, and even the smallest actions have an impact. I have a great deal of respect for every single entrepreneur who has taken the leap into small business ownership and wakes up every day seeking to make a positive impact, whether that is for customers, staff, family or a wider stakeholder network.

If you follow the process I've outlined in this book, you are guaranteed to be in a better position in a year's time. You'll not only have begun achieving the goals you have set out to achieve, but you'll do it with clarity and with confidence.

To your success.

INDEX

THE
**VERY
GOOD**
COMMUNITY

Where entrepreneurs experiment, learn and grow — together

It's an amazing time to be an entrepreneur. It's never been easier to dream, do and grow on your own with access at your fingertips to everything you will ever need.

And I love the term **'entrepreneur'** because it's limitless. If you are self-identifying as an entrepreneur, you **are** an entrepreneur. If you're building a business, you're an entrepreneur.

But building a successful, profitable and **growing business** is a bit of a different story.

Entrepreneurs that grow successful and profitable businesses are financially rewarded by their hard work. They have plans in place that help them thrive. They use their time precisely and they consume information that will help them get exactly where they want.

The most successful entrepreneurs learn from the best and take action based on results.

That's why we built **The Very Good Community.**

Inside The Very Good Community, we're a group of entrepreneurs running experiments, learning from each other, learning from experts and implementing The Very Good Marketing framework from the ground up. Not only will The Very Good Community encourage you to grow smarter and faster, but you also get the opportunity to learn from one another and be supported along the way.

If you're serious about growing your business, join us today!

verygoodmarketing.com.au/ community

Printed and bound by CPI Group (UK) Ltd, Croydon, CR0 4YY

23/06/2023

03229810-0001